Books of the Old Testament

Torah ("the Law")
Genesis
Exodus
Leviticus
Numbers
Deuteronomy

Traditionally, Joshua, Judges, Samuel and Kings are included in the Prophets, while Daniel, Ruth and Esther are included in the Writings.

Writings

History:
Joshua
Judges
ʷRuth
1 & 2 Samuel
1 & 2 Kings
1 & 2 Chronicles
Ezra
Nehemiah

Wisdom and Poetry
ʷEsther
ʷJob
ᵖPsalms
ʷProverbs
ʷEcclesiastes
ᵖSong of Songs
ʷ*Wisdom literature*
ᵖ*Poetry*

Ruth and Lamentations are shown in the order they appear in the Bible ("canonical order").

Ruth and Esther easily cross genres between History and Wisdom

The Prophets
Isaiah
Jeremiah
ᵖLamentations
Ezekiel
Daniel
Hosea
Joel Amos
Obadiah
Jonah
Micah
Nahum
Habakkuk
Zepheniah
Haggai
Zechariah
Malachi

} 12 "Minor Prophets"

Books of the New Testament

Gospel Accounts:
Matthew
Mark
Luke
John

Acts of the Apostles

Letters:
Romans
1 & 2 Corinthians
Galatians
Ephesians
Philippians
Colossians
1 & 2 Thessalonians
1 & 2 Timothy
Titus
Philemon   } Letters of Paul
Hebrews
James
1 & 2 Peter
1, 2 & 3 John
Jude

Revelation

The Apocrypha (or "Deuterocanonical Books") *see page 38*

Tobit
Judith
Additions to Esther
Wisdom
Ecclesiasticus (*Sirach*)
Baruch

Letter of Jeremiah
Additions to Daniel:
 -Song of the Three Jews
 -Susanna
 -Bel and the Dragon
1 & 2 Maccabees

The Orthodox sometimes add:
Prayer of Manasseh
1 & 2 Esdras
Psalm 151
3 Maccabees

A Tour of the Bible

An Introduction for the Unfamiliar

by Tom Pumphrey

Copyright © 2015 by Tom Pumphrey

Blue Kayak Publishing, LLC, Roswell, Georgia, USA.
www.bluekayakpublishing.com
All rights reserved.

Scripture quotations marked "NRSV" are from the *New Revised Standard Version of the Bible,* copyright 1989 by the Division of Christian Education of the National Council of the Churches of Christ in the USA. Used by permission. All rights reserved.

Scripture quotations marked (NIV) are taken from the Holy Bible, New International Version®, NIV®. Copyright © 1973, 1978, 1984, 2011 by Biblica, Inc.™ Used by permission of Zondervan. All rights reserved worldwide. www.zondervan.com The "NIV" and "New International Version" are trademarks registered in the United States Patent and Trademark Office by Biblica, Inc.™

Regarding material on page 71: Supplementary Material Taken from the New Revised Standard Version Bible, copyright © 1996 the Division of Christian Education of the National Council of the Churches of Christ in the United States of America. Used by permission. All rights reserved.

ISBN: 978-0-9963003-0-8

Library of Congress Control Number: 2015906205

To the Glory of God

The Rev. Tom Pumphrey studied Mechanical and Aerospace Engineering at Cornell University, and worked for the Lincoln Electric Company for over twelve years in sales and product management. He managed a sales territory in St. Louis, Missouri and became a Product Manager in the company's Automation Division at their headquarters in Cleveland, Ohio. In 2001, he entered Virginia Theological Seminary in Alexandria, Virginia, graduating with honors in 2004, and was ordained a priest in the Episcopal Church that year.

He became the rector (pastor) of St. Mark's Church in Honey Brook, Pennsylvania until 2009. From 2009 to 2013 he was an Associate at St. David's in Wayne, near Philadelphia, focusing primarily on Discipleship ministries. Tom became well known in the Diocese of Pennsylvania for his teaching and consulting in the area of church leadership. He was a regular speaker at the annual Diocesan Vestry Symposium and he led a popular six part series of classes on Leadership Development for the Church. In the parish, he focused on survey courses of basic Christian teaching, such as the basics of the Bible, the Creeds, and learning about the various Christian denominations and their histories. In 2013, Tom became the rector of the Episcopal Church of St. Peter and St. Paul in Marietta, Georgia. Tom is married and has two sons. This is his first book.

Here are more responses to *A Tour of the Bible*:

"In an era when biblical literacy cannot be assumed, Tom Pumphrey has provided a helpful resource for the new reader of the Bible seeking a basic engagement with the contents of the most revered book in history. Fashioned to provide quick confidence, it will raise your cultural literacy by exposing you to the most resonating passages of scripture and may just awaken your faith that you too may be able to hear and understand the Word of God."
—*Rev. Dr. Timothy P. McConnell, Eastminster Presbyterian Church, Marietta, GA*

"It gives me tremendous joy to receive a working copy of the new book, *A Tour of the Bible: An Introduction for the Unfamiliar*. I took a quick read of it and was immensely impressed by its effective pedagogical design, its concise survey of biblical contents, and its rich resources and aids for critical reading of the Bible. It is certainly a brilliant and enticing "tour map" drawn by an experienced tour guide with passion and wisdom. The 50,000 Foot Fly-by followed by the Section-by-Section tour lands logically on the Greatest Hits and this sequence guides the readers to approach the Scripture in proper contexts and helps them to hear God's voice in and through biblical texts. The charts and maps are extremely useful for any readers wishing to understand the big picture and thematic contour of the Bible, including leaders of Bible study groups and seminarians preparing for GOE's. The final chapters on analytical methods, interpretive worldviews, and reading strategies, though brief, provide practical guidance that will help serious students of the Bible to think critically on the challenging and transforming word of God. Tom has made an invaluable contribution to the church with this gem-packed book."
—*The Rev. John Y. H. Yieh, Ph.D. Molly Laird Downs Professor of New Testament, Virginia Theological Seminary*

Preface

Since the days I trained customers and sales people for the Lincoln Electric Company, I have enjoyed teaching. Entering ordained ministry is all the more rewarding, since I learn as I teach, and share in discovering the wonders of Almighty God and the story of God's people. From 2004 to 2009, I was the rector of St. Mark's Episcopal Church in Honey Brook, and from 2009 to 2013, I was an associate at St. David's in Wayne—both churches in Chester County, Pennsylvania, outside of Philadelphia. Part of my vocation in each parish was teaching adults on Sunday mornings, or in special evening or weekend programs. I put together a number of survey courses that reviewed the basics of Christian teaching, including the basics of the Bible.

In 2011, as a follow-on program to Alpha, we offered an eight week series introducing the Bible. Handouts from earlier classes and new handouts for this class formed a booklet that became the basis for *A Tour of the Bible*. We tested this material in further introductory classes and in a weekly Bible Study that surveyed the Greatest Hits. Participants received the booklet with great enthusiasm.

Many people in the pews are self-conscious about their knowledge of the Bible. They feel timid and insecure and wish they knew more but are embarrassed to ask. These courses and that booklet helped a number of people feel more grounded and gave them a framework for listening to the lessons in church or engaging in small group studies. With the encouragement of my rector, the Rev. W. Frank Allen, I began to shape this booklet into a book for the public. After the delay of moving to become the rector of St. Peter and St. Paul in Marietta, Georgia, it was time to publish *A Tour of the Bible*.

I pray that this resource is helpful for you as you seek to understand the Bible and to hear God's voice speaking in its pages. I have learned so much from this project and there is always more to learn—especially from those who use this book. I would be so privileged to receive any feedback and suggestions that you might have for improvements.

Great thanks to Tim Morrison for editing my manuscript, to the Rev. Hillary Raining, Justin Streeter and others for their encouragement in this project, to the members of the "Walking Through the Bible" Bible Study at St. David's, and to Joey Mayes for his excellent design work on the maps and cover. Thanks to my wife Silke and our sons Alex and James for their patience and support for this and all my ministries, and to my dad, the Rev. David W. Pumphrey, whose legacy I am so very privileged to inherit. Thanks above all to a generous God without whom my efforts would be fruitless. May God go ahead of me to prepare and bless all who use *A Tour of the Bible*.

Tom Pumphrey
Advent, 2014

Books of the Old Testament

Torah ("the Law")
Genesis
Exodus
Leviticus
Numbers
Deuteronomy

Traditionally, Joshua, Judges, Samuel and Kings are included in the Prophets, while Daniel, Ruth and Esther are included in the Writings.

Writings

History:
Joshua
Judges
ʷRuth
1 & 2 Samuel
1 & 2 Kings
1 & 2 Chronicles
Ezra
Nehemiah

Wisdom and Poetry
ʷEsther
ʷJob
ᵖPsalms
ʷProverbs
ʷEcclesiastes
ᵖSong of Songs

ʷ*Wisdom literature*
ᵖ*Poetry*

Ruth and Lamentations are shown in the order they appear in the Bible ("canonical order").

Ruth and Esther easily cross genres between History and Wisdom

The Prophets
Isaiah
Jeremiah
ᵖLamentations
Ezekiel
Daniel
Hosea
Joel Amos
Obadiah
Jonah
Micah
Nahum
Habakkuk
Zephaniah
Haggai
Zechariah
Malachi

} 12 "Minor Prophets"

Books of the New Testament

Gospel Accounts:
Matthew
Mark
Luke
John

Acts of the Apostles

Letters:
Romans
1 & 2 Corinthians
Galatians
Ephesians
Philippians
Colossians
1 & 2 Thessalonians
1 & 2 Timothy
Titus
Philemon
Hebrews
James
1 & 2 Peter
1, 2 & 3 John
Jude

} Letters of Paul

Revelation

The Apocrypha (or "Deuterocanonical Books") *see page 38*

Tobit	Letter of Jeremiah	*The Orthodox sometimes add:*
Judith	Additions to Daniel:	Prayer of Manasseh
Additions to Esther	-Song of the Three Jews	1 & 2 Esdras
Wisdom	-Susanna	Psalm 151
Ecclesiasticus (*Sirach*)	-Bel and the Dragon	3 Maccabees
Baruch	1 & 2 Maccabees	

Table of Contents

Map of Ancient Near East: ....Inner Front Cover
Map of Ancient Israel and Judah: ....Inner Front Cover
Chart of the Books of the Bible ....Facing Inner Front Cover
Preface 1

Part I: Orientation
Introduction: Why and How to Use this Book 4
How Do We Use the Bible? 5
How to Get Started Reading the Bible 6
The 50,000 Foot Fly-by: the Basic Narrative, Structure and Dates 8
A Taste of the Bible: (samples of different kinds of Biblical literature)......................11
Special Bible Vocabulary 12

Part II: Section by Section Tour
Old Testament
Torah (Genesis, Exodus, Leviticus, Numbers, Deuteronomy) 14
History (Joshua, Judges, Ruth, Samuel, Kings,
    Chronicles, Ezra, Nehemiah, Esther)..18
(Ruth and Esther easily cross genres with Wisdom; see below)
Poetry Books (Psalms, Song of Songs, Lamentations)..24
    Understanding Hebrew Poetry throughout the Old Testament......................25
    More on the Psalms 28
Wisdom (Ruth, Esther, Job, Proverbs, Ecclesiastes)...30
Prophets (Isaiah, Jeremiah, Daniel, Ezekiel, and the 12 Minor Prophets).................32
The Apocrypha..38
The New Testament
The Gospel Accounts (Matthew, Mark, Luke, John) 40
Acts of the Apostles 46
Letters of Paul (Romans through Philemon) 48
Hebrews and the General letters (James, 1 and 2 Peter, 1, 2, and 3 John, Jude) 54
Revelation 56

Part III: Resources for Further Learning 57
Guide to Translations and Editions of the Bible..58
How Did the Bible Become the Bible? 60
Analytical Methods...62
Interpretive "World-views" that Influence How We Understand the Bible....................64
Reading Strategies (tables of what to read when) 65
Additional Resources (annotated Bibliographies and references) 74
Glossary 76
Index...82

Map of New Testament Cities and Regions: ....Inner Back Cover
Map of First Century Judea and Samaria: ....Inner Back Cover

Part I: Orientation

Introduction: Why and How to Use this Book

A Tour Guide

Many people are unfamiliar with the Bible or are mystified by its contents. Once the staple of Western culture, fewer people now read the Bible or have much exposure to it. Even churchgoers hear segments of scripture on Sunday morning, but often do not know the context or how to follow the story line. Who are these people with strange names? How do we read and understand the Bible and how can we hear God speaking to us today through this book of ancient books? On a trip to a foreign country, with different languages, climate and culture, many of us are confused until we get a tour, a map, a taste of the food and some orientation about how to approach this new land. The same is true when we read the Bible.

An Overview

This book seeks to provide that orientation to Holy Scripture and to help people hear the voice of the living God from its pages. This book can be a reference book to help you get your bearings, or it can provide a systematic introduction. We start with a "50,000 Foot Fly-by," and continue with outlines of the basic story line in the Bible, section by section. Along the way, you will also find references to specific passages that provide a taste of each section, without requiring reading the whole thing. These appetizers are called "The Bible's Greatest Hits" because they are the most interesting and influential passages. These lists help you to find the gems amidst the genealogies.

Part I provides a basic orientation: This section provides brief introductions of how the Bible is used, how it is structured and how to start to read the Bible. You then find a "50,000 Foot Fly-by" to get a sense of the big picture and the basic story line of the Bible. There is also a section on a handful of key words to understand when reading the Bible.

Part II begins a section-by-section tour of the Bible. For each section, you will find an outline, a list of "Greatest Hits" to read, an overview of the basic story line in that section, and a helpful summary of each Biblical book in that section—reviewing the story and the message.

Part III then provides resources for further learning, including guides to different translations and editions of the Bible, a section on how the Bible became the Bible, discussions of analytical methods, and worldviews that impact how we understand the Bible. There is also a section on strategies for daily or weekly reading of the Bible, and lists of additional resources for how you can learn more. The inside covers provide conveniently located references: a chart of the Bible's books facing the inside front cover, and maps of Bible lands inside front and back covers.

I hope that this book will be a helpful reference to you as you read the Bible prayerfully, listening for God's voice and seeking the guidance of the Holy Spirit.

How Do We Use the Bible?

Perhaps that is an odd question, but it is an important place to start. Some people use the Bible as a list of rules. Others use it as a book of quaint stories, others as an archaeological artifact, and still others as a geological record. Perhaps these descriptions paint caricatures too dramatically, but with such different expectations of the Bible, readers are even more easily confused. The Bible is a complex text—a collection of numerous ancient texts, each of them complex in their own right. We read English translations from ancient and extinct languages (even modern Hebrew and Greek are new constructions of the old languages). The characters and contexts are so different from our own time. And the *kinds* of literature are varied and serve different purposes. The task of understanding the Bible is not so simple.

A Theological Text

Understanding how we *use* the Bible makes a huge difference in the task of *understanding* the Bible. **This book takes the approach of treating the Bible as a theological text**—a text of religious claims and accounts of experiences of God in history. This may sound like an obvious approach, but many studies of the Bible operate on far more secular assumptions. Secular study of the Bible tends to focus on reconstructing the events with secular criteria, including the assumption that God never is involved in the world—that supernatural events simply *can't* take place.

This may be a helpful assumption in the secular world that seeks an objective view outside of religious conversation. But the Bible is indeed a religious text. The Bible has been influential in the world precisely as a religious text—as the "Word of God." Secular scholarship has yielded some important insights to the Bible, and this book will make use of those insights. But the concerns of secular introductions often miss the basic story of what the text says and what it means to Christians (and in the case of the Old Testament—to Jews as well). I hope that the reader (atheist and believer alike) will find this introduction helpful as a way of understanding how the Bible is read and understood and influential to Christians. Such an endeavor will help mutual understanding among religions more than an archeological reconstruction.

So How Do Christians Use the Bible?

- **The primary use of the Bible for Christians is to hear the voice of the living God, through the power of the Holy Spirit, revealing Jesus Christ, the true "Word of God," who himself reveals God the Holy Trinity.**
- The Bible is the primary historical witness to Israel's experience of God, to the life, death and resurrection of Jesus Christ, and to the early church's experience of Jesus, the Holy Spirit and God the Father.
- Since the early days of the church, the Bible is the "canon of Holy Scripture," the authoritative body of texts for Christians, and the sacred basis for our theology and living.
- The Bible is authoritative on the character and identity of God and our relationship with God.
- The Bible is authoritative on our character and identity as people and as God's people.
- We call the Bible "the Word of God" because its writers were uniquely inspired by the Holy Spirit. The Bible is very complex and reflects different times and contexts, but we still believe that God speaks to us today through the Bible.
- Notice that we do not, for instance, use the Bible as a geology textbook, though we recognize history where the writer has an historical purpose.

The best way to read the Bible is prayerfully, together with other Christians, listening for the voice of the living God. The Holy Spirit speaks through the church—the community of Christians around us and from Christian history too, helping us to listen and read rightly.

How to Get Started Reading the Bible

The best way to read the Bible is with a group of people with whom you can prayerfully discuss and engage the text. But some people need the basic background that helps orient them to the discussion. So what is the best way to tackle reading the Bible on your own?

Which Bible to Read?
First, you will need a Bible. Any trip to the library or bookstore can be overwhelming with the variety of Bibles being offered. You will find an alphabet soup of alternatives: KJV (King James), NIV, NRSV, NASB, NAB, etc… If you have no idea how to choose between translations, see page 58 in Part III for a ***Guide to Translations and Editions of the Bible***. This guide will give you brief descriptions of a number of translations available, and help you understand the differences between them. Usually there is a compromise between accuracy and ease of reading. Try to find the balance that is most helpful for you. I often recommend the NIV or NRSV translations. The ESV is another good translation gaining popularity.

A "study" Bible with footnotes, margin notes, maps, introductions, etc, can be very helpful in understanding the text. These notes offer interpretations from the bias of the authors and publishers, but they can often clarify what may be confusing in the text.

Navigating the Bible
This may sound silly, but first: *find the table of contents*! Most beginners do not know how to find the book of Obadiah any more than they can find Romans or Psalms. And this is a big book through which to go hunting! Find the table of contents and mark it with a sticky-note so that you can find it more easily as you go.

Chapter and Verse
After you find the book within the Bible, you still need to find the particular passage. Hundreds of years after the Bible texts were written, someone divided the material in each book into chapters. Each sentence or phrase was then numbered into verses. So "John 3:1-16" means "the book John, chapter 3, verses 1 through 16." This numbering system makes it easier to find particular passages.

Where to Begin? What (in this Huge Book) Should I Read First?
To the unfamiliar, the Bible is a large and intimidating book. How does one get started? Many people choose the obvious place: the beginning. Genesis opens with creation and moves forward in a somewhat chronological order. However, the Bible doesn't always read like a novel. Legal material and (notoriously) long genealogies appear in the midst of the stories. Political details and inheritance documents can bog down a reader eager for plot. Long portions of prophetic denouncements in Hebrew poetry can become exhausting to the newcomer. Even in the New Testament, complex theological discourse can be a challenging starting point for the beginner.

There may be better options for the beginner than simply reading the book straight through. Any reading strategy will take some time as well. Here are key questions to ask:
- How much time do I want to take?
- How much detail can I absorb?
- What kind of literature or which sections are most interesting to me?

Reading Strategies for Individual Study

Using this Book to Read through the Bible
"A Tour of the Bible" is designed to be a resource to guide you through the Bible. You can use it along side of your reading, as a tourist might refer to a map as she walks through town. Or you might use it as a guide book, starting with this book, and reading the recommended scripture passages. These lists of "Greatest Hits" include over 130 passages particularly important, memorable or helpful in representing a Biblical book. This will expose you to the basic story of scriptures and some of the key passages. If you read along with *"A Tour of the Bible,"* the comments, notes, and guides will help you get your bearings as you read. If you take this approach, you can go at your own pace and read what interests you. Or you can try two "Greatest Hits" per day. If you read every weekday, you can cover the material in roughly three months.

Bible Reading on Your Own: Strategies for Getting Started
One strategy is to read the Bible in multiple cycles—starting with a light sampling, then starting over with a new plan that adds more material. With each cycle, names and places will become more familiar, and the new material will have a better context. Then you can try tackling the whole Bible. In Part III of this book, you will find details on how to employ the strategies listed below. Review this list to see which one is best for you, and look in Part III for more details.

<u>**Strategies to Get Started with Portions of the Bible:**</u>

- **20 Bible Basics:** a starter sampler of twenty key passages (see page 65)
- **Greatest Hits:** 130 brief passages (each taking roughly 7 minutes to read) (see page 66)
  Read the 46 asterisked passages in one month, 2 readings (15 minutes) per weekday
  Read all 130 passages in three months, 2 readings (15 minutes) per weekday
- **An introduction with five whole books of the Bible:**
    - Matthew (the story of Jesus)
    - Genesis (creation and the Hebrew ancestors)
    - Acts (the birth of the church)
    - Ruth (a short Old Testament story of fidelity)
    - Philippians (a New Testament letter about joy in Christ)
- **Three two-week courses,** a chapter a day on either Jesus, Paul or an introduction to the Old Testament (see page 71)
- **Reading Most of the Bible** (abridging the Old Testament; see page 72)

<u>**Reading all of the Bible in one to three years:**</u>

There are numerous resources available to guide you through reading the whole Bible over a period of time—from start to finish or moving around in a comprehensive sampling. These are sometimes called *lectionaries*, calendars that schedule particular passages for each day. There are three year lectionaries, two year lectionaries, and one year lectionaries. The shorter the time usually means two to three separate readings each day. However, you can use these lectionaries to make your own plan. Many lectionaries still leave out large portions (similar to the abridgment of the Old Testament strategy on page 72). One useful resource is the "One Year Bible," a book with all of the Biblical passages laid out in a 365 day plan. For more on lectionaries, see page 73.

A 50,000 Foot Fly-by: the Basic Narrative and Structure

Literary Outlines: Old Testament and New Testament

There are two main subdivisions in the Bible: The Old Testament and the New Testament. Some have questioned these names, but the names have stuck in most conversations. The Old Testament is the collection of books sacred to Jews. The Old Testament *was* the Bible for Jesus and his disciples. The early Christian church read from it in worship and taught from it. But they also read from writings of the apostles—the leaders among Jesus' followers. These writings became what we call the New Testament, thereby giving name to the "old" one.

The Old Testament
The Old Testament constitutes roughly 75% of the volume of the Bible. It contains a variety of kinds of literature—from story and poetry to law and history. Its basic frame is the history of God's relationship with his people Israel. There is poetry and wisdom literature, and books from the prophets, proclaiming God's word to the people. And there are laws of their covenant relationship with God.

The basic story starts (in Genesis, the first book) with God creating the world and relating to it and to humanity, caring for people and dealing with their sin. Then we read stories of the ancestors of the Jews: Abraham, Isaac and Jacob (the "patriarchs") and their families. God chooses them for a unique relationship with him. In the book Exodus, the story continues with God using Moses to deliver them from slavery in Egypt. God makes a covenant (like a contract or promise) with them that is described in the Ten Commandments and several books that expand these laws. This is why the first five books are often called the Law (the **Torah**).

The history of Israel continues with the establishment of Israel as a nation, the first kings (including King David and King Solomon), then the division of Israel into two kingdoms: Israel in the north and Judah in the south. The prophets write in challenge to the evils of the kings and peoples of this several hundred years period. The kingdoms are destroyed by larger empires, Assyria and Babylon. This destruction and the exile to Babylon is presented as part of God's judgment and renewal of the people. The people later return to the land once more.

The literary structure and diversity of the Old Testament
The Old Testament was written in Hebrew (with a little Aramaic) over numerous centuries. The Old Testament contains three kinds of texts: the **Torah**, the **Prophets**, and the **Writings**. The Torah is the central core of texts sacred to Jews, though they also use the Prophets and the Writings. These last two categories are less defined terms. Traditional groupings of Prophets and Writings don't necessarily match genres as expected. Writings include **History, Poetry** and **Wisdom** literature. Ruth and Esther could fall into either categories of history or wisdom.

Old Testament:
- Torah: Genesis, Exodus, Leviticus, Numbers, Deuteronomy (the first five books)
- Prophets: Isaiah, Jeremiah, Ezekiel, Daniel and the twelve "Minor Prophets"
- Writings:
    History: Joshua, Judges, (Ruth), Samuel, Kings, Chronicles, Ezra, Nehemiah, (Esther)
    Poetry: Psalms, Lamentations, Song of Songs
    Wisdom: Ruth, Esther, Job, Proverbs, Ecclesiastes

> *Traditionally, Joshua, Judges, Samuel and Kings are included in the Prophets, while Daniel, Ruth and Esther are included in the Writings.*

The New Testament Story and Literary Structure:
The New Testament contains scriptures revered by Christians, written in Greek by the early followers of Jesus. They tell the story of the life, death and resurrection of Jesus (through four writers or traditions in the **"Gospel"** accounts), the story of the early church, and records of letters and teachings for the church in the first century AD. The New Testament books can be grouped as **Gospels** and **Letters** (also called "Epistles"), with the Acts of the Apostles as a sequel to the Gospel according to Luke, and with Revelation as an apocalyptic text (visionary prophecy). The book Hebrews is also more of a sermon than a letter, but it is traditionally grouped with the Letters.

New Testament:
- Gospels: "according to…" Matthew, Mark, Luke and John: Jesus' life, ministry and the cross.
- Acts of the Apostles: account of the Apostles, stressing the Holy Spirit ("part II" of Luke).
- Letters: letters by Paul to various churches; Hebrews (a sermon), and other letters.
- Revelation: apocalyptic literature: prophecy in vivid visionary form about God's victory.

The Apocrypha or Deutero-canonical books
Note: the Apocrypha is a selection of Jewish literature that is not held as authoritative scripture by Protestant Christians (nor included in Hebrew scriptures by Jews). For this reason, these books are sometimes omitted from editions of the Bible, and sometimes included in a separate section to distinguish them. Eastern Orthodox and Roman Catholic Christians *do* include the Apocryphal books (sometimes called the "Deutero-canonical" books) in their Bibles. Some Bible editions therefore integrate these books into the Old Testament, and others maintain them in a separate section. See the chapter on the Apocrypha on page 38 for more info.

See the next page for historical outlines of the Bible and key historical dates.

Historical outlines:

Here, in a few words, are the basic historical frameworks for the Old and New Testaments:

The Old Testament:

Creation and patriarchs, EXODUS→ Judges, Kings (Israel and Judah)→ EXILE, return.

The timeframe of the Old Testament story spans over 1000 years from the patriarchs (Abraham, Isaac and Jacob) to the return from exile. **The Exodus** (where God delivered the Hebrews from slavery in Egypt and brought them to the Promised Land) **and the Exile** (where Babylon destroyed Jerusalem and its holy temple, and carried plunder and people into exile) are the two monolithic events in the Old Testament. Added to the destruction of the rebuilt Jerusalem temple by Rome in AD 70, and the Nazi Holocaust, these are the big events in Jewish history.

After the exodus, the tribes lived loosely in the land, and leadership was provided by "judges" as needed. The tribes were united into one kingdom under King Saul (then David and Solomon). Under Solomon's son, the kingdom split into two kingdoms: Israel and Judah (north and south). Israel was destroyed by Assyria, and Judah was destroyed and exiled by Babylon, the people later returning and rebuilding the temple under the rule of the Persian Empire. The Prophets spoke against the evils of the kings and people especially during the time of the kings.

The New Testament:

Jesus and the early church that followed.

The timeframe of the New Testament, by contrast, spans only decades. The New Testament describes the birth, ministry, death and resurrection of Jesus and the early decades of the church that followed. These books were written between ~AD 50 (early letters) to ~AD 100 (Gospel according to John and Revelation). The Gospel accounts most certainly had oral origins and their final forms probably derived from combinations of earlier writings in some cases.

Key Biblical Dates:

~1400-1300 BC:	Exodus from Egypt.
~1000 BC:	Kings: Saul, David, and Solomon.
922 BC:	The Kingdom divides into Israel (north) and Judah (south).
721 BC:	Assyria destroys Israel and scatters the people.
586 BC:	Babylon destroys Jerusalem and the Temple, and takes people into exile.
538 BC:	First return of Jews from exile (under the Persians).
~450 BC:	Temple rebuilt under Ezra; Walls of Jerusalem rebuilt under Nehemiah.
167 BC:	Maccabean revolt and Jewish independence (Rome later gains control).
~30 AD:	Ministry, Crucifixion and Resurrection of Jesus.
70 AD:	Rome destroys the Temple and scatters the Jewish people (the "Diaspora").

A Taste of the Bible:

The Bible is a book of books. Though inspired by one God, these books were written by many authors across centuries, and with different styles and purposes. Notice the difference in the genre of literature in the following passages:

- Genesis 1:1-2:3 — A more theological and structured account of creation.
- Genesis 2:4-3:7 — A more personal account of creation.
- Genesis 10:11-27 — Genealogy.
- Genesis 39 — Narrative.
- Leviticus 2:4-10 — Legal code.
- 1 Kings 15: 1-9 — Historical chronicle.
- Psalm 51:1-13 — Poetry: A psalm of lament.
- Psalm 100 — Poetry: A psalm of praise.
- Proverbs 10:1-9 — Proverbial wisdom.
- Ecclesiastes 2 — Wisdom philosophy.
- Jeremiah 2:1-24 — Prophecy: Speaking the word of the LORD.
- Matthew 13:3-9 — Parable.
- Mark 14:55-64 — Historical account.
- Romans 5:12-21 — Theological discourse.
- Philemon — A letter: The whole book is one short chapter.
- Revelation 21:10-14 — Apocalyptic: Visionary prophecy.

We expect different kinds of meaning from different genres. For instance, a verse that says "God is a rock" sounds more like metaphor in a poem rather than a piece of systematic theology. However, "crucified under Pontius Pilate" in a historical account is more for the record than for theological metaphor.

Special Bible Vocabulary

Some words in the Bible have loaded or special meaning. If you are interested, review some of these words below:

The Lord: When you see this word printed in all capitals in the Old Testament, this is a substitute for the Hebrew word that is the "divine name"—the name of God, most notably revealed to Moses in his encounter with God in the burning bush. The Hebrew letters of this word (יהוה) are usually transliterated as YHWH. Some Bible translations might render this as "Yahweh." But, as the Ten Commandments remind us, we are not to "take the name of the Lord your God in vain." The ancient and generally current practice is, therefore, not to pronounce this name at all, but rather to use a substitute word. Using Yahweh does not follow this rule—Jews do not use Yahweh. "Jehovah" (deriving from translators' mistakes) is even worse.

When Jews read the Hebrew scriptures and encounter this name, they do not pronounce it, but rather say aloud *adonai* which is the Hebrew word for "Lord." The ancient Greek translation of the Old Testament (from before Jesus' time), rendered the divine name into the Greek word for Lord. Calling Jesus "the Lord" is therefore not simply a comment about his authority, but also a comment about his divinity.

To distinguish the divine name from the regular Hebrew word for lord, English translations use all capitals for the divine name: "the Lord." Sometimes you will read "The Lord God" with "God" in all capitals. This is an attempt by the translators to render a phrase that uses the word adonai and the divine name together ("The lord YHWH"). The Hebrew word otherwise translated "God" (without capitals) is *Elohim*. El is a short form and appears in words and names that refer to God, such as Bethel (*Beth-El* = house of God).

"I am" or "I am he": Remember Moses and the burning bush? He asks for God's name and God replies "I am who I am… say to the Israelites 'I am has sent me to you.'" The word or phrase "I am" in Hebrew is very, very close to the letters of the divine name (see above). This comes up in the Gospel accounts, especially in John, where Jesus will from time to time use this phrase "I am." It's harder to tell in English, but there are times where this emphasis stands out, such as his arrest in the Garden of Gethsemane (John 18:1-8). Jesus is implying that he is God.

The nations: The Hebrew word for "nations" is the same word that means "Gentiles." So listen for the implications whenever you read or hear anything about "the nations." This isn't just a political or broad statement, it implies "those other people who aren't God's people." This can be hostile, or it can be in various statements that promise God's blessings on "the nations."

Israel: This is the name given by God to Jacob, Isaac's son (and Abraham's grandson). The word means "one who wrestles with God." The early references to the nation of Israel (since they referred to nomadic tribes) really refer to the collection of Jacob's descendants, grouped in twelve tribes, each based on descendants of Jacob's twelve sons.

Later, when the unified nation of all the twelve tribes split in two, the nations were called Judah (in the south, with the tribes of Judah and Benjamin) and Israel (in the north—the ten remaining tribes). At that time, the name Israel was more politically specific. The Jews are more specifically descendants of Judah. But they are also the children of the original Israel—the people of Jacob.

Heart: The heart in the Hebrew world is the place of thinking. The gut is the place of feeling.

Brother: Fellow Christians were "brother" or "sister" to each other, showing the church to be a new family to the believer. It could mean "church member," but with far more intimacy.

Covenant: As in current legal jargon, a covenant is a kind of contract. But a covenant is more involved—it is a whole person commitment, generally a lifelong commitment, such as the Baptismal Covenant, or the Marriage Covenant. The Old Testament describes how God made covenants—with Noah, Abraham, and with the people of Israel delivered from Egypt. The verb for making a covenant is literally "to cut." Ancient covenant-making ceremonies involved cutting up animals to demonstrate "so may it happen to me if I break this covenant." A covenant is binding on both parties, and calls them into a particular kind of relationship. The primary covenant with God is "I will take you as my people and I will be your God." (Exodus 6:7a, NIV).

Breath, Wind, Spirit: These three words translate a single word in Hebrew (*ruach*) or a single word in Greek (*pneuma*). Keep this in mind when you hear such phrases as "the spirit of God was hovering over the waters" [in creation] (Genesis 1:2b, NIV). This especially stands out in Ezekiel's vision of the dry bones: "prophecy to the breath… say to the breath…come from the four winds, O breath, and breathe into these slain that they may live." (Ezekiel 37:9, NIV). There are often double or triple meanings involved.

Loving-kindness, or Steadfast-love: These compound words are English translators' attempt to create a code word for the Hebrew word *chesed* (pronounced with a guttural, throat-clearing sound at the beginning: "*KHESS-ed*"). This word signifies a kind of love that involves covenant-faithfulness—a heartfelt, whole-person, commitment-love. Sometimes this gets translated "mercy" as in the King James Version of Psalm 23 "surely goodness and mercy shall follow me all the days of my life." The word mercy in this translation is actually *chesed*—God's committed, covenant, steadfast-love.

Servant, Slave: These two English words translate the single word in Hebrew (*eved*) or in Greek (*doulos*). Context will often communicate the difference between service or bond-slavery. But often the situation of servant or slave was so very similar. The NRSV translation of the Bible tends to prefer the word slave in all cases, but I find that a bit distracting, since it carries so much emotional weight and historical baggage for Americans.

Word: There are multiple words for "word," both in Hebrew and Greek. One of these words in each language carries extra meaning—a meaning of power to do something (such as "God said 'let there be light,'" or "the word of the LORD came to the prophet Ezekiel…"). In Greek, this is expanded in Plato's philosophy. Plato departed from the standard polytheism of Zeus and Athena, etc, to claim one almighty power—perfect and ideal and utterly separate from the material world we inhabit. But how does this one God create? Through his Word—"***Logos***" in Greek. Christians used this philosophy to describe Jesus' divinity. Jesus is the divine *Logos* of the Father—the divine Word of God. This is best described in the opening of the Gospel according to John: "In the beginning was the Word, and the Word was with God and the Word was God. He was with God in the beginning. Through him all things were made; without him nothing was made that has been made…. The Word became flesh and made his dwelling among us…" (John 1:1-3, 14a, NIV).

Love: There are several Greek words for love, including *philia* for brotherly love, and *agape* for selfless love. Paul commonly stresses agape, which is often translated "charity" from the Latin *caritas*. Think of this when you hear 1 Corinthians 13 ("love is patient, love is kind…").

Messiah: means "anointed" (in Greek: "Christ"). Israel made kings by anointing them with oil.

Part II: Section by Section Tour
The Old Testament: The Torah

Outline of the Torah: the First Five Books

Genesis: Beginnings and Patriarchs: creating, relating, and choosing
- 1-6: Creation and Fall
- 6-11: Noah and Ancestors
- 11-25: Abraham, Sarah and Isaac
- 25-36: Jacob
- 37-50: Joseph

Exodus: God saving and making a covenant with his people
- 1-15: Moses and the Exodus
- 15-18: In the Wilderness
- 19-24: The Ten Commandments and Covenant Making
- 25-40: Details for Worship (32-34: wilderness trouble)

Leviticus: The Laws of sacrifice and holiness

Numbers: Journey in the Wilderness (with lists of people)
- 1-10: Census
- 11-25: Wilderness Journey and some Laws; Balaam: 22-24
- 26-36: Census, Inheritance Details, some Laws

Deuteronomy: Torah laws and review of the covenant
- 1-3: Preface
- 4-11: Ten Commandments and Exhortations
- 12-26: Law Codes
- 27-34: Epilogue

> Referred to as "The Law" in the New Testament, the word "torah" means "instruction." It is the core of the covenant between God and his people.

Greatest Hits of the Torah!

* **Genesis 1:1-2:3**: Creation
  Genesis 2:4-25: God makes man and woman in his image
  Genesis 3: "The Fall:" Adam and Eve sin against God
  Genesis 6:5-9:17: Noah and the flood, and God's covenant
  Genesis 12:1-7: The Call of Abram
  (See the whole Abraham saga, Genesis 12-25)
  Genesis 22:1-18: The "sacrifice" of Isaac
* **Genesis 32:22-32:** Jacob wrestles with God and becomes "Israel"
  (See also the whole Joseph saga, Genesis 37-50)
* **Exodus 3:1-15** [and more in 3:16-4:17]: Moses and God at the burning bush
  Exodus 12:1-14: The first Passover
* **Exodus 20:1-20:** The Ten Commandments
  Numbers 11:4-30: Grumbling in the wilderness and God providing for them (this is hilarious)
  (see also Numbers 22-24: Balaam refuses to curse Israel; Balaam's donkey)
  Deuteronomy 5:1-21: A second rendition of the Ten Commandments
* **Deuteronomy 6:1-9:** The Great Commandment (also the "Shema," Israel's basic creed)
  Deuteronomy 30:11-20: "See, I have set before you life and death…choose life"

> **Exhortation** is a kind of speech that strongly encourages and urges the listener to a specific course of action.

Overview of the Torah

The first five books of the Bible are known as The Torah (also called **"The Law"** in the New Testament, the **"Pentateuch"** by some scholars, and sometimes **"the five books of Moses"**). The Torah is the central body of holy scriptures for Jews (the other Old Testament books are important, but secondary). Starting with creation, **Genesis** then describes God establishing the people of Israel from their ancestors Abraham, Isaac and Jacob. Genesis ends with Jacob's extended family moving to Egypt to join Jacob's son, Joseph. Generations later, the Hebrews are enslaved in Egypt, and **Exodus** tells the story of God saving them out of Egypt under the leadership of Moses. This is the first act of the covenant God makes with them. Their part of the covenant is to keep the torah—the law. They receive the Ten Commandments and the law from God, and wander in the wilderness before coming to the Promised Land. **Leviticus** and **Deuteronomy** expand on the law, and **Numbers** expands on the story of their time in the wilderness (Numbers also includes a lot of census information). See the review of each book below.

The text of the Torah took shape in ancient oral and literary traditions. A close reading of the text suggests that there may have been multiple traditions that were carefully preserved and woven together in the text we have now. The final form of the Torah may have involved compiling and editing before and after the Exile (587 BC). See Source Criticism, page 62.

Genesis

Beginnings: Genesis begins with creation. Other ancient religions described the sun, moon and stars as gods themselves. In Genesis, these are merely lights in the sky that God creates, All creation is pronounced good, and human beings (in contrast to claims of other pagan religions) are the pinnacle of God's creation—in relationship with God. But soon things fall apart, as the man and woman rebel against God and sin mars this creation. Cain (Adam and Eve's son) kills his brother Abel, and the generations that follow continue their evils. God sends a destructive flood, and calls Noah to build an ark to preserve mating pairs of animals to start anew. When the waters recede, God makes a covenant with Noah never again to destroy the world in flood, with the rainbow as a sign of this covenant.

Patriarchs: The narrative then shifts to the account of the Hebrew patriarchs and matriarchs: the first ancestors of Israel. God calls Abraham and Sarah out of Mesopotamia to the land of Canaan (present day Israel). God promises that their descendants will become a great nation. Decades later, they are still childless, but God renews this promise several times. Abraham has a son by Sarah's servant Hagar, but finally their son Isaac is born to Sarah. They send Hagar and her son Ishmael away, and God promises to make them a great nation as well (they are described as the ancestors of the Arabs). God asks Abraham to be willing to give up even Isaac, and Abraham proves willing, almost sacrificing his son. But God intervenes, clarifying that no human sacrifice shall be made to the Lord (unlike in other religions).

Isaac and his wife Rebecca have two sons: Esau and Jacob. Jacob cheats his brother of his birthright, and runs away to stay with a relative. He prospers there and marries two women, Rachel and Leah (monogamy had not yet become the standard). Jacob's craftiness continues until he leaves to return to Canaan and face his brother. On the way, Jacob wrestles with God and God changes Jacob's name to Israel, meaning, 'one who wrestles with God.' Jacob and his brother are then reconciled.

The Twelve Tribes and Joseph: Jacob/Israel has twelve sons—these are the ancestors of the "twelve tribes of Israel." The story of these sons, Joseph in particular, then fills the last 14 chapters of Genesis. The brothers despise Joseph as his father's favorite, and they sell him into slavery in Egypt. But "The Lord was with Joseph" and he prospers, becoming chief of Egypt's grain storehouses. When famine hits Canaan, his brothers go to Egypt to buy grain. With great drama, the brothers are eventually reconciled. The family all relocates to Egypt, setting the stage for the Exodus.

Exodus:

Generations later, Israel's descendants have become numerous, and are enslaved by Pharaoh, the king of Egypt. Moses grows up in Pharaoh's palace, but later flees Egypt. He encounters God in a bush that burns, yet is not consumed. Here the Lord tells Moses to go to Pharaoh and lead his people out. Moses is rather reluctant at first, yet he goes. Pharaoh will not relent until, after ten plagues afflict Egypt, he finally tells them to go. The last plague is death. The angel of death passes over the houses of the Hebrews, as they eat the first "Passover" meal. As the people flee, Pharaoh sends his army in pursuit. God separates the waters of the sea to let the Hebrews pass through to Sinai, and he drowns the Egyptian army when they try to follow.

Wilderness and Covenant: The people then wander in the wilderness for a generation. The wilderness journey is not easy. Despite God delivering them from slavery, the people often grumble. God provides for them water and "manna" (bread from heaven) and quail. God makes a covenant with them—he will be their God and they will be his people. The core of the covenant is the "Shema" (see **Deuteronomy** below) and the Ten Commandments (listed in both Exodus 20 and Deuteronomy 5), but the law is expanded in Exodus, **Leviticus** and **Deuteronomy**. See the outlines for more information. The law can be very detailed, in part because it contains case law—how to solve disputes about cattle, etc. The law also serves the purpose of distinguishing the people as God's people.

Leviticus:

This book, dealing with the laws of the Levites (the tribe of priests), concerns the laws of sacrifice and holiness—what is "clean" and "unclean" in preparation for worship, or in general as a people set apart to be God's people.

Numbers:

This book is named Numbers because of long census lists, detailing the twelve tribes. The middle section of Numbers contains an excellent narrative describing the wilderness wanderings—where the people grumble against God, yet God provides for them anyway. They follow a pillar of fire by night, and a pillar of smoke by day as God leads them.

Deuteronomy:

The title of this book means "second law." This is a re-telling of the covenant making, and a review of the law. See in particular, chapters 5 and 6—the Ten Commandments and the Shema—the central creed for Jews (The Lord your God is one, and you shall love the Lord your God with all your heart and soul and strength). The Torah ends with a renewal of the covenant before the entry into the Promised Land (which starts in Joshua).

Chart of Abraham's Family Tree

The Old Testament is primarily the story of God and the descendants of Abraham, his son Isaac and his grandson Jacob (also known as Israel). Here is Abraham's Family Tree:

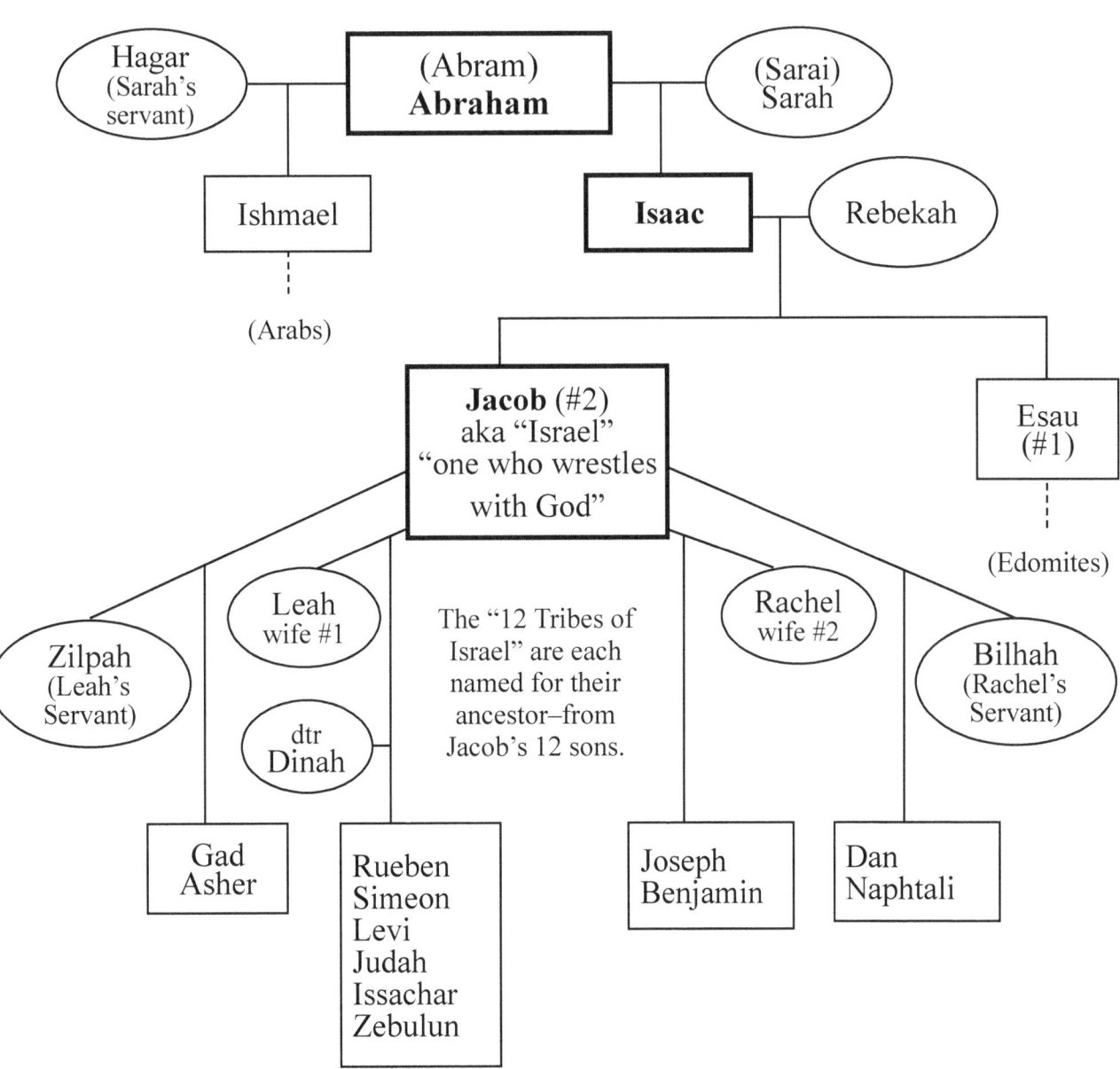

Jacob ("Israel"):

2 wives: Leah & Rachel (Jacob favored Rachel)
2 surrogate wives—each a servant of a wife
    12 sons => the "Twelve Tribes of Israel" (and a daughter Dinah)
    Most beloved: sons of Rachel: Joseph and Benjamin
        Tribe of Judah: …David…Jesus
        Tribe of Levi: …Moses and Aaron…priests

The Old Testament: History of Israel

Outlines: History of Israel

Joshua: Conquest of Canaan by the "12 Tribes"
- 1-12: Conquest
- 13-24: Reorganization

Judges: Stories of 12 Heroes who fought for the tribes before the monarchy (with a sense of a downhill slide in their characters) Including: Deborah (4-5), Gideon (6-8) and Samson (14-16). The tribes then deteriorate from there (17-21)

Ruth: a short story of a Moabite woman adopted into Israel (see also Wisdom literature)

1 & 2 Samuel: Origins of the monarchy
- 1-7: The Prophet Samuel
- 8-15: Saul as King
- 16-31: David and Saul
- 2 Sam: David's reign

1 & 2 Kings: History of the monarchy to the destruction of Jerusalem
- 1-11: Solomon
- 12- 2 Kings 17: The Divided Kingdom (Israel in the north and Judah in the south)
  - Note: 1 Kings: 17-19, and 2 Kings: 1-2: the Prophet Elijah and King Ahab
  - Note: 2 Kings: 2-9: The prophet Elisha
- 2 Kings 18-25: The last years of Judah

1 & 2 Chronicles: History of the monarchy (parallel to Kings)
- 1-9: Introduction
- 9-29: David
- 2 Chronicles 1-9: Solomon
- 10-28: The Divided Kingdom
- 29-56: The last years of Judah

Ezra: Return and rebuilding the temple after the Exile

Nehemiah: Rebuilding the walls of Jerusalem

Esther: a story of fidelity to the Jews in the face of persecution (see also Wisdom literature).

Greatest Hits of the History of Israel!

Joshua 24:14-24: The people renew the covenant ("as for me and my house, we will serve the LORD")

Judges 4: a sample of a hero story from Judges: Deborah

Ruth 1:5-18: Ruth and Naomi

* **1 Samuel 3:** The call of Samuel

1 Samuel 16:1-13: Samuel anoints David

1 Samuel 17: David and Goliath

* **2 Samuel 11- 12:23:** David and Bathsheba

* **2 Samuel [18:4-15], 18:24-33:** David mourns for his son Absalom, who rebelled against him.

1 Kings 15:25-26: An example of a formula for most of each king in Israel or Judah: "…and he did what was evil in the sight of the LORD…"

* **1 Kings 19:1-15:** Elijah meets God, not in earthquake, wind or fire

Esther 4:8-16: 'Perhaps you [are here] for just such a time as this'

Esther 7:2-6: Esther finally accuses Haman

The Ancient Near East

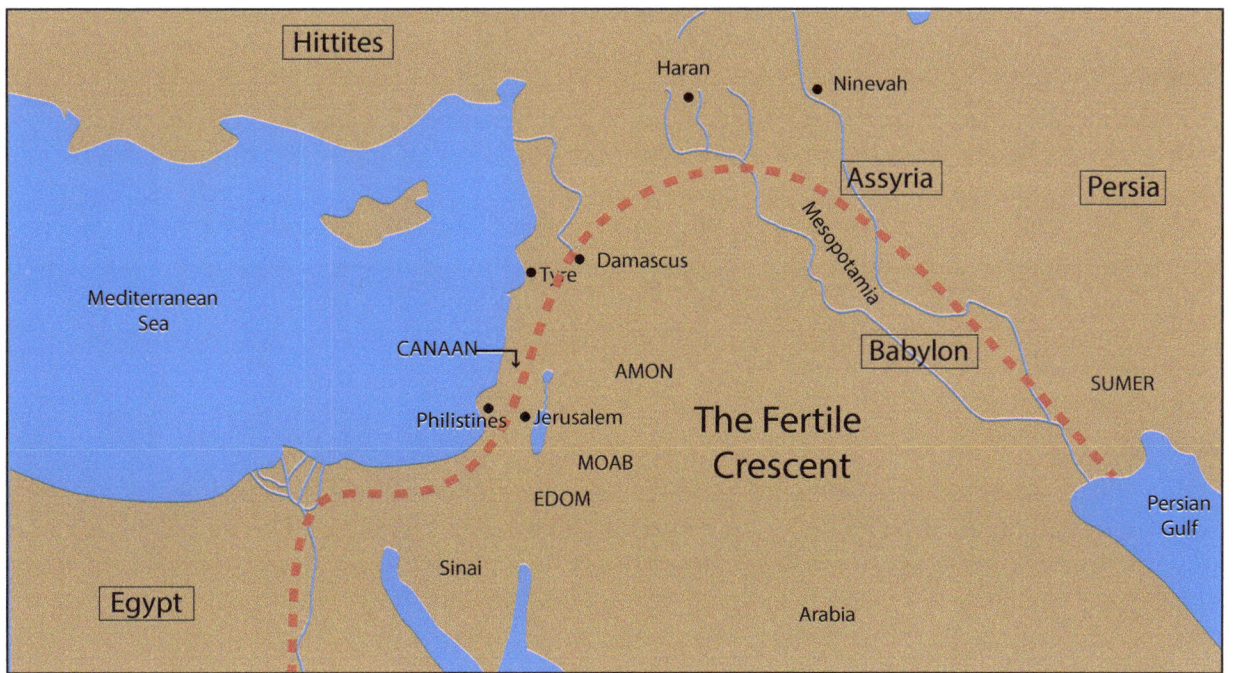

The Hebrews repeatedly were caught between Egypt and the empires of the east in the Fertile Crescent. Israel in the north was destroyed by Assyria, and Judah by Babylon.

Overview of the History of Israel

Ten of the next eleven books of the Bible after the Torah recount the History of Israel, from the entry into the Promised Land, to the return after the exile in Babylon. However, these history books are primarily concerned with the state of the people's relationship with God. International politics only matter though the lens of the covenant. Though the books **Ruth** and **Esther** are not so much history literature (see Wisdom, p.30), they are placed in the Bible in chronological order (Ruth is an ancestor to David; Esther is set in the exile under Persia).

Conquest, Judges and Kings: Joshua leads the people from the wilderness into the Promised Land, where by God's protection and strength alone, they defeat their enemies, renew the covenant, and settle in the land. They live as loosely affiliated tribes, relying on heroes known as "**Judges**" to rouse the people to action when their enemies threaten them. But the character of these Judges seems to go downhill as time goes on—only their reliance on The Lord helps them. Eventually, the people ask for a king through the prophet **Samuel**. God gives them Saul to be king, and later David, uniting the twelve tribes. David is a central figure in the History of Israel and their relationship with God. David's son King Solomon builds the temple in Jerusalem.

Divided Kingdom: After Solomon, the kingdom divides into Israel in the north, and Judah in the south. **Kings** and **Chronicles** repeatedly cite king after king who "did evil in the sight of the Lord, even greater than his father before him…" They turned toward other gods and oppressed the people. Prophets, such as Elijah and Elisha arose to challenge the infidelity of the Kings and people. Occasionally there was a good king, such as Josiah, who instituted religious reforms in Judah. Ultimately, their infidelity was their downfall. Israel was destroyed by the Assyrian Empire, and Judah was destroyed by the Babylonian Empire. Jerusalem was destroyed and most importantly, the temple was destroyed (a huge blow to the people who identified the temple with God's presence). The elite were carried off into exile in Babylon, later returning when the Persians took power over Babylon (**Ezra** and **Nehemiah** lead the rebuilding).

Overview of Each Book of the History of Israel

Joshua:

Joshua describes the conquest and reorganization of the Promised Land under Moses' successor, Joshua. As the battles are recounted, the issue for the text is not so much the political gains or strength of the people, as it is the sovereignty of God in their endeavors. If they rely on God, they will prosper. If they seek their own gain, they suffer defeat. The famous battle of Jericho (chapter 6) is a case in point. The walls of Jericho come down not through strength of arms, but only after the people complete a march around the city each day for a week in a series of rituals. When their enemies are defeated, the Hebrews settle by tribes in the land and live as a loose tribal confederation.

Judges:

While Joshua describes a blanket victory, Judges describes ongoing struggles with local kingdoms that remain, especially the sea peoples known as the Philistines. During this period, when trouble or conflict arose, God would raise up a champion to rouse the people and lead them against their enemies. When these "judges" were faithful to God, they would find success. When they strayed or sought their own glory, however, disaster would follow. Chapter one reviews the basic pattern, followed by accounts of twelve judges.

These include Deborah, who is unique as a female leader, and the only judge described as resolving disputes. Gideon is called to lead an increasingly smaller army to victory so that they realize that they win only by God's strength and not by their own strength. Gideon's son tries to proclaim himself king, with disastrous results. Several other judges follow, ending with Samson. Samson's strength comes from his vow to the Lord, a vow symbolized by not cutting his hair. His weakness for violence and women (especially Delilah) undo him. After Samson, the book of Judges tells a story of horrific evils and bloodshed among the tribes, returning to a common refrain "In those days, Israel had no king; everyone did as he saw fit."

Ruth:

Not strictly a piece of history literature (see the section on Wisdom literature), Ruth is a four chapter long story of Ruth, a foreign (Moabite) woman adopted into Israel by her mother-in-law Naomi. Ruth says famously "where you go, I will go…your people will be my people and your God my God" (Ruth 1:16). God provides for her, and she marries a man named Boaz. Ruth becomes an ancestor to King David and, through Joseph, to Jesus.

1 Samuel:

Samuel is all one book, most likely divided onto two scrolls due to its size. 1 Samuel tells of the prophet Samuel, and the establishment of the monarchy over the twelve tribes: first king Saul, then King David. Samuel is called as a prophet from before his birth. When the people ask God for a king, God reluctantly agrees—but with warnings about the evils of kings (since God should be their true king). Samuel anoints Saul with oil (this is how kings were made), and Saul is successful. When Saul disobeys God, Saul falls from God's favor. Samuel finds David and anoints him. However, many years pass before David assumes the throne. David fights the Philistine champion Goliath (by God's strength alone) and takes a role in Saul's court. Saul becomes jealous, and David flees into the wilderness. David never tries to harm Saul since Saul is the Lord's anointed king. Eventually Saul dies in battle, and David then takes the throne.

Ancient Israel and Judah

2 Samuel:

Much of 2 Samuel details David establishing his reign as king over all Israel. David is described as "a man after God's own heart." But David has his troubles too and soon his family problems occupy the narrative. David commits adultery with Bathsheba, sending her husband Uriah to his death in battle. In a brilliant scene of speaking truth to power, the prophet Nathan calls David to account for his sin. The rest of David's family (rather large, due to his many wives) fares no better. One son, Amnon, rapes his half-sister Tamar. Another son, Absalom, then kills Amnon, and later rebels against David to take the throne. Absalom is killed in battle, and David mourns for the loss of his son. All this foreshadows God's grief for his wayward people.

1 and 2 Kings:

Solomon: Kings, like Samuel and Chronicles, is one book, divided due to size. Kings continues the narrative of Samuel, charting the rest of the kings through to the destruction of Jerusalem. Solomon takes over from his father David, and his reign is characterized by splendor and prestige. Solomon asks God for wisdom, and God honors his request with both wisdom and riches. But Solomon's many wives and many foreign wives lead him astray. When he dies and his son takes the throne, the kingdom is divided: Judah in the south and Israel in the north.

Divided Kingdom: Kings then describes each reign in each kingdom, often introduced with "and he did evil in the sight of the Lord…" The kings allowed worship of pagan gods such as Baal and Asherah, and oppressed the people. The people were often unfaithful too, turning to these pagan gods and idol worship rather than staying true to the covenant. Prophets spoke out against kings and people. Occasionally there is a good king, such as Josiah, who led religious reforms. But his successors strayed again, and within 30 years, Judah was destroyed.

Defeat and Destruction: The Bible presents Assyria and Babylon as agents of God's judgment, calling his people back to himself. Assyria destroyed Israel and displaced its people in 722 BC. Judah was destroyed—including Jerusalem and its temple—by Babylon in 586 BC. This was a horrifying defeat: the temple is the place where God is present; how could the Lord allow this defeat? The prophets deal further with this question, but the book of Kings blames this defeat on repeated infidelity to God.

Prophets: Among the accounts of the kings, there are longer stories of some characters, such as the prophets Elijah and Elisha. Each of these preached against Ahab, King of Israel, and his pagan wife Jezebel. Elijah and Elisha perform miracles (such as healing, sustaining food, fire from heaven to defeat the prophets of Baal) and denounce the Baal worshippers and their leaders.

1 and 2 Chronicles:

Chronicles parallels Kings as a history of the monarchies (1 Chronicles just for David). David is presented without his sins, and the centrality of temple worship is of key importance. God's sovereignty again takes precedence in all things.

Ezra:

After Persia conquers Babylon, King Cyrus allows exiled Jews to return to the land and re-occupy Jerusalem. They begin to rebuild the temple and under the leadership of the priest Ezra, attempt to purify themselves as a people wholly devoted to the Lord. Includes many lists…

Nehemiah:

Ezra and Nehemiah were likely part of the same book, originally (and likely compiled by the same hand that wrote or edited Chronicles). Nehemiah was the governor of Judah during this period, and led the rebuilding of the walls of Jerusalem.

Esther:

Like Ruth, Esther is a book that straddles genres of History and Wisdom literature (see more in the Wisdom section). Esther is (secretly) a Jew who becomes Queen to the Persian king Artaxerxes II (404-358 BC) during the time when the exiles were returning to Jerusalem under Persian rule. Haman is a courtier who sets out to persecute the Jews, especially Esther's cousin Mordecai. Esther boldly steps in to foil his plans and defend her people in a beautiful and well crafted narrative. The Jewish holiday Purim has its origins in this story.

Kings in Israel and Judah (all dates are BC)

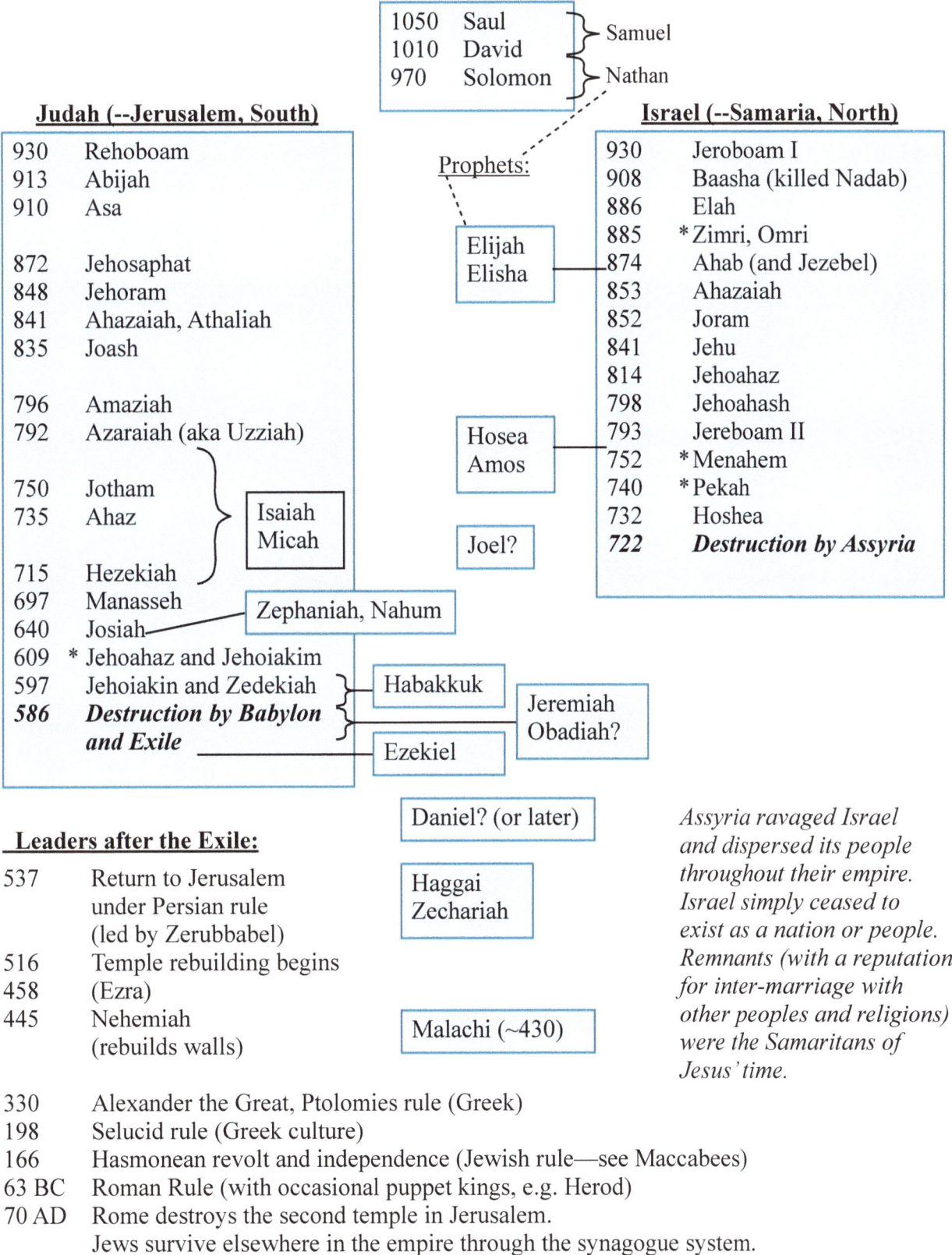

1050	Saul	— Samuel
1010	David	
970	Solomon	— Nathan

Judah (--Jerusalem, South)

930	Rehoboam
913	Abijah
910	Asa
872	Jehosaphat
848	Jehoram
841	Ahazaiah, Athaliah
835	Joash
796	Amaziah
792	Azaraiah (aka Uzziah)
750	Jotham
735	Ahaz
715	Hezekiah
697	Manasseh
640	Josiah
609	*Jehoahaz and Jehoiakim
597	Jehoiakin and Zedekiah
586	**Destruction by Babylon and Exile**

Prophets:

Elijah / Elisha

Hosea / Amos

Joel?

Isaiah / Micah

Zephaniah, Nahum

Habakkuk

Ezekiel

Jeremiah / Obadiah?

Daniel? (or later)

Haggai / Zechariah

Malachi (~430)

Israel (--Samaria, North)

930	Jeroboam I
908	Baasha (killed Nadab)
886	Elah
885	*Zimri, Omri
874	Ahab (and Jezebel)
853	Ahazaiah
852	Joram
841	Jehu
814	Jehoahaz
798	Jehoahash
793	Jereboam II
752	*Menahem
740	*Pekah
732	Hoshea
722	**Destruction by Assyria**

Leaders after the Exile:

537	Return to Jerusalem under Persian rule (led by Zerubbabel)
516	Temple rebuilding begins
458	(Ezra)
445	Nehemiah (rebuilds walls)

Assyria ravaged Israel and dispersed its people throughout their empire. Israel simply ceased to exist as a nation or people. Remnants (with a reputation for inter-marriage with other peoples and religions) were the Samaritans of Jesus' time.

330	Alexander the Great, Ptolomies rule (Greek)
198	Selucid rule (Greek culture)
166	Hasmonean revolt and independence (Jewish rule—see Maccabees)
63 BC	Roman Rule (with occasional puppet kings, e.g. Herod)
70 AD	Rome destroys the second temple in Jerusalem. Jews survive elsewhere in the empire through the synagogue system.

* A couple of brief reigns in either kingdom are omitted. OT Dates from Edwin Thiele.

Old Testament: Hebrew Poetry

Poetry is found in most Old Testament books, especially the Prophets. Three books are exclusively poetry: Psalms, Song of Songs and Lamentations. These overviews serve better than outlines for these collections of poems. **See the special section on the Psalms on p.28.**

Overview of Poetry Books:

Psalms:

Located in the Bible after Nehemiah, Esther and Job, and before Proverbs, the Psalms are the pinnacle of Hebrew poetry, used extensively in Jewish and Christian worship. These 150 psalms are arranged in five sections, though there are generally no obvious themes to these sections until the last section (107-150), clearly dominated by praise. All the sections present a mix of different types of psalms: "Royal" psalms (about the king), psalms of Lament, Praise and Thanksgiving, and "Imprecatory" psalms: inviting God's aid against enemies. See p. 28.

Song of Songs:

Located after Psalms and Proverbs, and before Ecclesiastes, the Song is a somewhat steamy love poem, interpreted by the church as either a sign of marital love or as an allegory of God's love for his people (better yet, both). This book is sometimes called the Song of Solomon, with Solomon assumed as the groom. The eight chapters present five encounters and a conclusion.

Lamentations:

Located between Jeremiah and Ezekiel, these are five poems dramatically lamenting the destruction of Jerusalem and the people.

Greatest Hits of Old Testament Poetry!

How can one choose from among the psalms?? All the Psalms are one giant Greatest Hit. Most Christians read from the Psalms in every worship service.

Psalm 1: Their delight is in the law of the Lord …
Psalm 22: My God, my God, why have you forsaken me?
*****Psalm 23:** The Lord is my shepherd
*****Psalm 40:** I waited patiently upon the Lord
*****Psalm 42:** As the deer longs for the water-brooks, so longs my soul for you, O God
Psalm 46: God is our refuge and strength (cf. Luther: "A Mighty Fortress is our God")
Psalm 51: Have mercy on me, O God
Psalm 90: Lord, you have been our refuge
Psalm 95: Come, let us sing to the Lord
Psalm 96: Sing to the Lord a new song
Psalm 100: O be joyful in the Lord all you lands
Psalm 130: Out of the depths I have called to you, O Lord
*****Psalm 139:** Lord, you have searched me out and known me
Psalm 150: Praise the Lord!
Song of Songs 2:10-13: Set me as a seal upon your heart
Song of Songs 8:6-7: Many waters cannot quench love
Lamentations 1: How lonely sits the city that was once full of people…
See also Exodus 15:1-21 (the songs of Moses and Miriam)

Hebrew Poetry as a Genre throughout the Old Testament

Several books of the Bible are predominately Hebrew Poetry.
In fact, the size of all of Old Testament poetry is larger than the entire New Testament.

Psalms and Songs:
- Psalms
- Song of Songs (love poetry)
- Lamentations (lamentation of the exile)

Wisdom:
- Most of Proverbs
- Much of Ecclesiastes (reflections on the struggle of life)
- Most of Job (reflections on calamity and God's sovereignty)

Prophets:
- Most prophetic writing is in poetic form
- The exceptions include most (but not all) of: Ezekiel, Haggai, Zecharaiah, Daniel and Jonah (the last two are more narrative than prophetic in form).

Prose is more conscious of its words than common speech. As a further step beyond prose, in poetry, the *expression* of the message is of great importance. The expression can itself convey content. Poetry tends to be more terse, more compact, and therefore more packed with further implications and meaning than prose.

Hebrew Poetry is very different from our English idea of poetry. Hebrew poetry is not based on rhyme or meter, though there are occasional rhythmic patterns. Hebrew poetry is mostly distinguished by "thought rhymes:" parallel lines of comparison, contrast, or intensification. Consider the same concept expressed in prose or in poetry:

Judges 4:19 (NRSV):
> *Then he said to her, "Please give me a little water to drink; for I am thirsty." So she opened a skin of milk and gave him a drink and covered him.*

Judges 5:25 (NRSV):
> *He asked water and she gave him milk,*
> *She brought him curds in a lordly bowl.*

Hebrew Poetry is usually expressed in couplets or triplets of lines. The most common form is a pair of parallel phrases:

> *Praise the LORD, all you nations; ***
> *laud him, all you peoples.* (Psalm 117:1, Book of Common Prayer)

Sometimes, the couplets present contrast:

> *A wise child makes a glad father,*
> *but a foolish child is a mother's grief.* (Proverbs 10:1, NRSV)

One scholar describes the form as "A, and what's more, B"
> *Smoke rose from his nostrils*
> *and a consuming fire out of his mouth; ***
> *hot burning coals blazed forth from him.* (Psalm 18:9; notice three lines in this case)

Hebrew Poetry in the Prophets

(notice how some "orphans" without a pair stand out rhetorically):

Isaiah 40 (in the King James Version, memorable for fans of Handel's Messiah):
> *¹ Comfort ye, comfort ye my people, saith your God.*
> *² Speak ye comfortably to Jerusalem,*
>   *and cry unto her, that her warfare is accomplished,*
>   *that her iniquity is pardoned:*
>
> *for she hath received of the L<small>ORD</small>'s hand double for all her sins.*
>
> *³ The voice of him that crieth in the wilderness,*
> *Prepare ye the way of the L<small>ORD</small>,*
> *make straight in the desert a highway for our God.*
>
> *⁴ Every valley shall be exalted,*
>   *and every mountain and hill shall be made low:*
>
> *and the crooked shall be made straight,*
>   *and the rough places plain:*
>
> *⁵ And the glory of the L<small>ORD</small> shall be revealed,*
>   *and all flesh shall see it together:*
>
> *for the mouth of the L<small>ORD</small> hath spoken it.*

Amos 5:21-24 (NRSV):

> *²¹ I hate, I despise your festivals,*
>   *and I take no delight in your solemn assemblies.*
>
> *²² Even though you offer me your burnt offerings and grain offerings,*
>   *I will not accept them;*
> *and the offerings of well-being of your fatted animals*
>   *I will not look upon.*
>
> *²³ Take away from me the noise of your songs;*
>   *I will not listen to the melody of your harps.*
>
> *²⁴ But let justice roll down like waters,*
>   *and righteousness like an ever-flowing stream.*

Hebrew Poetry in Wisdom Literature:

Proverbs: advice of wisdom in poetic form. Here are proverbs from chapter 10 (NRSV):

> *⁹ Whoever walks in integrity walks securely,*
> > *but whoever follows perverse ways will be found out.*
> *¹⁰ Whoever winks the eye causes trouble,*
> > *but the one who rebukes boldly makes peace.*
> *¹¹ The mouth of the righteous is a fountain of life,*
> > *but the mouth of the wicked conceals violence.*
> *¹² Hatred stirs up strife,*
> > *but love covers all offenses.*

Ecclesiastes: Wisdom literature about folly in the struggles of life

Ecclesiastes 1:2-4 (NIV):
> *² "Meaningless! Meaningless!" says the Teacher.*
> *"Utterly meaningless! Everything is meaningless."*
> *³ What does man gain from all his labor at which he toils under the sun?*
> *⁴ Generations come and generations go, but the earth remains forever.*

Ecclesiastes 3:1-2 (NIV; notice that pairs parallel each other as well):
> *¹ There is a time for everything,*
> > *and a season for every activity under heaven:*
> *² a time to be born and a time to die,*
> > *a time to plant and a time to uproot,*

Job: Wisdom literature, mostly poetry, reflecting on calamity and God's sovereignty.

Job 38:4-5 (NRSV, God's reply to Job's complaint):
> *⁴ "Where were you when I laid the earth's foundation? Tell me, if you understand.*
> *⁵ Who marked off its dimensions? Surely you know!*
> *Who stretched a measuring line across it?*

Poetry in other books

Poetry often appears embedded in more narrative books. See the songs of Moses and Miriam in Exodus 15:1-21 (NRSV)

> *²¹ᵇ Sing to the LORD for he has triumphed gloriously;*
> *horse and rider he has thrown into the sea.*

Or the song of Deborah and Barak in Judges 5 (NRSV)

> *³ Hear, O kings; give ear, O princes;*
> *to the LORD I will sing,*
> *I will make melody to the LORD, the God of Israel.*

Or David's song of lament for Saul and Jonathan in 2 Samuel 1:19-27 ("how the mighty have fallen…") or other psalms in 2 Samuel 22 and 23.

The Psalms

The book of Psalms contains 150 Psalms arranged in five sections. Many, though not all, are attributed to David, but this may mean "about David" rather than written by him. Their writing, editing and compiling span a wide range of time periods. Many psalms are recognized as having a place in the liturgy of the people, as they do today. There are commonly recognized psalm forms: Royal Psalms, Psalms of Lament (individual and community), Psalms of Praise, Thanksgiving, and Imprecatory Psalms (asking God's aid against enemies). The Psalms are noted for their wide range of expression of God's initiative to us, and our human response to God, with all its emotional breadth. **Genre samples below** are from the Episcopal Church's Book of Common Prayer, 1979.

Royal Psalms, about the king (praise, commendation to God, coronation, wedding…)

Psalm 72: 1-4:
> *1 Give the King your justice, O God, **
>> *and your righteousness to the King's son;*
> *2 That he may rule your people righteously **
>> *and the poor with justice.*
> *3 That the mountains may bring prosperity to the people, **
>> *and the little hills bring righteousness.*
> *4 He shall defend the needy among the people; **
>> *he shall rescue the poor and crush the oppressor.*

Psalms of Lament: individual or communal psalms of lament. They often follow this form:
- Address to God
- Description of the trouble
- Petition/request
- Profession of trust in God
- Promise or Vow to God

Excerpts from Psalm 22:
> *1 My God, my God, why have you forsaken me? **
>> *and are so far from my cry*
>> *and from the words of my distress?*
> *2 O my God, I cry in the daytime, but you do not answer; **
>> *by night as well, but I find no rest.*
> *3 Yet you are the Holy One, **
>> *enthroned upon the praises of Israel.*
> *4 Our forefathers put their trust in you; **
>> *they trusted, and you delivered them.*

> *18 Be not far away, O LORD; **
>> *you are my strength; hasten to help me.*
> *19 Save me from the sword, **
>> *my life from the power of the dog.*
> *20 Save me from the lion's mouth, **
>> *my wretched body from the horns of wild bulls.*
> *21 I will declare your Name to my brethren; **
>> *in the midst of the congregation I will praise you.*

Psalms of Praise:

Psalm 150:
> *¹ Hallelujah! Praise God in his holy temple; **
>> *praise him in the firmament of his power.*
> *² Praise him for his mighty acts; **
>> *praise him for his excellent greatness.*
> *³ Praise him with the blast of the ram's-horn; **
>> *praise him with lyre and harp.*
> *⁴ Praise him with timbrel and dance; **
>> *praise him with strings and pipe.*
> *⁵ Praise him with resounding cymbals; **
>> *praise him with loud-clanging cymbals.*
> *⁶ Let everything that has breath **
>> *praise the L*ORD*! Hallelujah!*

Psalms of Thanksgiving:

Psalm 23:
> *¹ The L*ORD *is my shepherd; **
>> *I shall not be in want.*
> *² He makes me lie down in green pastures **
>> *and leads me beside still waters.*
> *³ He revives my soul **
>> *and guides me along right pathways for his Name's sake.*
> *⁴ Though I walk through the valley of the shadow of death, I shall fear no evil; **
>> *for you are with me; your rod and your staff, they comfort me.*
> *⁵ You spread a table before me in the presence of those who trouble me; **
>> *you have anointed my head with oil, and my cup is running over.*
> *⁶ Surely your goodness and mercy shall follow me all the days of my life, **
>> *and I will dwell in the house of the L*ORD *for ever.*

Imprecatory Psalms (asking God's aid against enemies):

Excerpt from Psalm 140:
> *⁷ O Lord G*OD*, the strength of my salvation, **
>> *you have covered my head in the day of battle.*
> *⁸ Do not grant the desires of the wicked, O L*ORD ***
>> *nor let their evil plans prosper.*
> *⁹ Let not those who surround me lift up their heads; **
>> *let the evil of their lips overwhelm them.*
> *¹⁰ Let hot burning coals fall upon them; **
>> *let them be cast into the mire, never to rise up again."*
> *¹¹ A slanderer shall not be established on the earth, **
>> *and evil shall hunt down the lawless.*
> *¹² I know that the L*ORD *will maintain the cause of the poor **
>> *and render justice to the needy.*

The Old Testament: Wisdom Literature

Outlines: Wisdom Literature

Ruth: [located earlier in the Old Testament, between Judges and 1 Samuel], Ruth is a short story of a Moabite woman, Ruth, adopted into Israel by her mother-in-law, Naomi. Ruth becomes an ancestor to David, and Jesus.

Esther: [located after the history books of Ezra and Nehemiah] Set in the reign of the Persian King Artaxerxes II (404-358 BC), during the Persian control of Judea.
Esther, a (secretly Jewish) queen to the Persian king, acts to protect the Jews from a plot against them by the evil Haman. This ends with the king protecting the Jews.
(The Jewish holiday Purim has its origins in this story).

Job: ponders the suffering of the righteous man, Job
- 1-2: Opening narrative: the setting of Job's tragedy
- 3-42: Poetic speeches by Job, his friends, and God (38-41)
- 42: Closing narrative of Job's restoration

Proverbs: [located after Psalms] Advice about the pursuit of wisdom ("the fear of the LORD is the beginning of wisdom"). 31 chapters in poetic form.

Ecclesiastes: Philosophical ponderings of the uncertainties of life (sometimes compared to a godly existentialism). "Vanity of vanity, all is vanity…" Best to fear and obey God and enjoy today.

Ruth and Esther cross genres between History and Wisdom (perhaps Daniel too). See more below.

The Apocryphal books include more wisdom literature, especially:
Wisdom:
- 1-6:21 Exhortation to Justice
- 6:22-10:21: in praise of Wisdom
- 11:1-19:22: The justice of God in the Exodus

Ecclesiasticus (also called "Sirach") is a loose collection of wisdom commentary.

Greatest Hits of Wisdom Literature!

Ruth 5:1-18: Ruth and Naomi

Esther 4:8-16 "Perhaps you [are here] for just such a time as this"
Esther 7:2-6 Esther finally accuses Haman

Job 1 and 2: the accuser defies God concerning Job. Job's sufferings.
*****Job 19:23-27:** Job's faith despite his suffering (part of Job's complaint)
Job 38:1-13: God's reply: "Where were you when I laid the foundation of the earth?"

Proverbs 10: A good sample of proverbs
*****Proverbs 31:10-31** the virtues of an excellent wife

*****Ecclesiastes 1:** "vanity of vanities! All is vanity"
Ecclesiastes 3:1-8: For everything there is a season
*****Ecclesiastes 12:13:** The heart of the matter

[**Wisdom 3:1-9:** The souls of the righteous are in the hand of God]
[**Ecclesiasticus** (Sirach) **44:1-15** "Let us now praise famous men"]

Overview of Wisdom Literature

Traditionally, the Old Testament is divided into Torah, Prophets and Writings. The "Writings" can then be classified into History, Poetry and Wisdom. But these classifications are more loose descriptions by scholars to help in the study of the Bible rather than strict divisions. Many books do not fall neatly into one category. There is a great deal of poetry in the Torah and especially the Prophets. Ruth and Esther have more style in common with Wisdom literature than the History books of Kings or Chronicles. Daniel and Jonah are counted among the prophets, but these books have more narrative than the other prophetic books, and less frequently follow the prophetic formula "thus says the LORD." Traditional lists place Ruth, Esther and Daniel among the Writings, and Joshua, Judges, Samuel and Kings among the Prophets.

Wisdom generally characterizes the books that emphasize practical living in response to God. Proverbs is the prototypical wisdom book: extolling wisdom and offering sage advice on how to live one's life. The Apocryphal/Deutero-canonical books Wisdom and Ecclesiasticus/Sirach generally follow Proverbs in form and focus. Ecclesiastes is similarly philosophical, but more reflective and less a collection of compact maxims than Proverbs. Job wrestles with tragedy in the lives of good people. Job is predominantly poetry, framed by narrative sections about Job's life. In the case of Ruth and Esther (and in the Apocrypha: Tobit and Judith), these books are all narrative and they deal less directly with God and more with human affairs.

Nonetheless, the "wisdom" in all these books is not a purely human wisdom (as current secular culture might envision it). Wisdom in the Bible has more to do with reverence to God than intelligence or brainpower. Wisdom involves choosing rightly as God's people. "The fear of the LORD, that is wisdom; and to depart from evil, that is understanding" (Job 28:28).

For summaries of <u>Ruth</u> and <u>Esther</u>, see pages 20 and 22 in the History Section.

<u>Job:</u> (located before Psalms)

The book Job is a lengthy reflection on bad things happening to a good person. The bulk of the book (chapters 3-42) is poetry: speeches by Job and his friends, and finally by God in reply. This poetic section is framed by two narrative sections. Job is a righteous man. Satan (the accuser) tells God that Job will drop his loyalty to God if Job's success in life goes away. Job then experiences disaster: the destruction of his family, and finally overwhelming disease. The speeches then follow. Job's friends insist that Job must have sinned. But Job stubbornly maintains his innocence and asks God for vindication. God's eventual reply suggests that God's ways are too mysterious for mortals. Job is humbled, and God finally restores Job's health, his fortune and his family.

<u>Proverbs:</u> (located after Psalms)

Traditionally ascribed to wise Solomon, these 31 chapters in poetic form praise the pursuit of wisdom (sometimes describing wisdom like a woman to be praised). Many proverbs present brief pieces of advice (often with strong contrast between wisdom and folly).

<u>Ecclesiastes:</u>

Traditionally ascribed to Solomon, Ecclesiastes is a more philosophical and perhaps a more cynical reflection on life—often compared to a godly existentialism. All our labors (in which we invest so much of our energy) are ultimately transient. Even our intellectual labors bring transient results. It is best to enjoy the gift from God that each day brings, to fear God (respect and honor God) and keep his commandments. "For apart from him who can eat or who can have enjoyment?" Ecclesiastes is partly prose and partly poetry.

The Old Testament: The Prophets

The Prophetic books are known in two groups: the "Major Prophets," whose books are long, and the "Minor Prophets" whose books are short. Their significance is far from minor! Some prophets appear only in the history narratives, especially the "Former Prophets" (see next page).

Outlines: The Major Prophets
(longer books than the minors)

Isaiah: In Judah: Judgment and messianic visions of restoration.
God's Judgment
- 1-6: Opening visions, rebuke and promise
- 7-12: Signs and warnings to Judah
- 13-23: Judgment on the Gentile nations
- 24-27: Judgment and blessing for all
- 28-33: Woes
- 34-35: Promise for God's people
- 36-39: Assyria and Babylon

God's Comfort
- 40-48: Restoration
- 49-57: The Suffering Servant
- 58-66: Ultimate deliverance and judgment

Jeremiah: Against the last kings of Judah, prophesying their doom through Babylon
- 1-35: Jeremiah's call, proclamations against Judah, and warnings of judgment
- 36-38: Jeremiah is persecuted
- 39-45: The last days of Jerusalem and the exile of the prophet
- 46-51: Judgment against the Gentile nations
- 52: A summary of the destruction of Jerusalem

Ezekiel: To the exiles in Babylon: Judgment and restoration
- 1-3: Opening visions and the call of Ezekiel
- 4-24: Judgment against Jerusalem (concerning its destruction and exile)
- 25-32: Judgment against the Gentile nations
- 33-48: Restoration from God (especially the dry bones vision in 37)

Daniel: Faithfulness to God in a pagan land; visions of God's victory
Daniel and his friends in Babylon
- 1: Daniel and friends succeed through their faithfulness
- 2: Nebuchadnezzar's dream and Daniel's interpretation
- 3: The great statue; Daniel's friends saved from the fiery furnace
- 4: Nebuchadnezzar's dream and exile (for blasphemy against God)
- 5: Belshazzar's Feast and the writing on the wall
- 6: Daniel in the Lion's Den

Apocalyptic visions
- 7-9: Visions
- 10-12: Predictions of future kingdoms, their blasphemy, and their downfall

Outlines: The Minor Prophets
(smaller books than the majors)

Hosea: Against Israel for their infidelity. Hosea uses a theme of being married to an unfaithful wife, yet seeking after her return.

Joel: Date and place unknown; God's call to repentance, and a vision of renewed people (invoked by the Apostles at Pentecost, when the Holy Spirit came upon them).

Amos: Against Israel for their oppression of the poor. "Let justice flow down like water, and righteousness like a mighty stream."

Obadiah Against Edom for not defending Judah; looking ahead to restoration.

Jonah: Narrative rather than prophecy: the reluctant, yet most successful prophet preaches to Ninevah. He's the one who gets stuck in the fish trying to escape God's call to prophesy, and can't understand God's mercy toward Ninevah.

Micah: In Judah; proclaims doom and hope during the time of Israel's downfall. Don't offer empty sacrifices while oppressing the poor, but "do justice, love mercy (*chesed*) and walk humbly with your God."

Nahum: In Judah, after Assyria destroyed Israel, proclaiming doom against Ninevah (Assyria's capital city).

Habakkuk: The prophet cries to God after the destruction of Jerusalem: "How long, O Lord, how long?" And God answers "Write the vision…"

Zephaniah: Against Judah's infidelity and against the Gentile nations, proclaiming the "day of the Lord" for judgment, and the renewal of the remnant.

Haggai: During the return after the exile. Haggai prophesies of the rebuilding of the temple and the restoration.

Zechariah: During the return from exile. Apocalyptic visions of the Messianic future and restoration of God's people.

Malachi: After the rebuilding of the temple. A rebuke for unfaithfulness, a call to repentance, and a look ahead to when God will come to purify his people.

The Former Prophets:

The books of Judges through Kings are sometimes called "the Former Prophets." The prophets in these books are known more for their actions and ministry than by record of their preaching (like the "Latter Prophets" of the majors and minors).

Samuel: (1 Samuel 1-24): the one who anoints Saul, and later David
Nathan: (2 Samuel 7 & 12, 1 Kings 1): Confronts David for his sin. Anoints Solomon
Elijah: (1 Kings 17 - 2 Kings 2): prophesies against Ahab and Jezebel (in Israel)
Elisha: (2 Kings 1-9): Continues after Elijah
  (There are many other prophets mentioned, but few others are remembered by name)

Greatest Hits for the Former Prophets:
* **1 Samuel 3:** The call of Samuel
  2 Samuel 12:1-23: Nathan confronts David over Bathsheba
* **1 Kings 19:[1-8], 9-15:** Elijah meets God, not in earthquake, wind or fire.
  2 Kings 5:1-16: Elisha and the healing of Naaman (a foreigner)

Greatest Hits of The Prophets!

Prophets speak the word of the LORD "Thus says the LORD ..."

Major Prophets:

   Isaiah 2:1-5: The vision of peoples streaming to the mountain of the LORD
* **Isaiah 6:1-8:** Isaiah's stirring vision of the throne room of God
   Isaiah 7:10-15: The prophecy of Immanuel: God with us ("behold, the virgin shall conceive..")
   Isaiah 9:1-7: "For unto us a child is born…wonderful, counselor, mighty God…"
   Isaiah 11:1-9: The branch of Jesse; the peaceable kingdom
   Isaiah 40:1-11: "Comfort ye my people…"
   Isaiah 53: The suffering servant
* **Isaiah 55**: Come, all you who are thirsty; my word will not go forth from me empty…

   Jeremiah 1:4-10: The call of Jeremiah ("but I am only a child…")
   Jeremiah 38: Jeremiah is thrown into a cistern, then brought out to warn the king
   Jeremiah 39:1-10: Jerusalem destroyed and exiled

   Ezekiel 1: vision of the Glory of the LORD (Ezekiel saw the wheel…)
   Ezekiel 2 [and 3]: The call of the prophet to speak to the exiles
* **Ezekiel 37:1-14:** The vision of the valley of dry bones returned to life
   Ezekiel 43:1-5: The Glory of the LORD returns to the temple

   Daniel 3: Faithful men delivered from the fiery furnace
   Daniel 5: Daniel interprets the writing on the wall
   Daniel 6: faithful Daniel delivered in the lion's den

The Minor Prophets (smaller books than the majors)

   Hosea 1:1-3, 2:11-3:1: The unfaithful wife abandoned, then brought back
   Hosea 8:7a: "They sow the wind, and reap the whirlwind."

   Joel 2:12-32: Call a fast; the LORD promises redemption and his Spirit on all people

* **Amos 5:21-24:** "Let justice roll down like water…"
   Amos 7:7-9, 8:1-7: A plumb line and a basket of fruit: the people's injustice

   Jonah 1: Jonah tries to flee from God (and winds up in the belly of a fish)
   Jonah 4: Jonah doesn't understand God's mercy

   Micah 6:6-8: "Do justice, love mercy, walk humbly with your God."

* **Habakkuk 1:1-6; 2:1-3:** "How long, O LORD, how long?" God answers "Write the vision…"

   Malachi 3:1-4: The day of the Lord: "and he shall purify the sons of Levi…"

Overview of the Prophets

Terms and Titles: A prophet is one who speaks a message from God. We sometimes think of prophets predicting the future (and that is true sometimes), but primarily, a prophet speaks the 'word of the Lord' for today. The most common formula is "Thus says the LORD …" There are classifications of prophets, but these terms apply to the books rather than the people. The "Former Prophets" are the books of Joshua through Kings, while the "Latter Prophets" are the books specific to the ministry of prophets themselves. Within the Latter Prophets are the "Major Prophets" and the "Minor Prophets." Again, these titles bear no reflection on the men, but rather on the length of their books: Major Prophets are long works, whereas the twelve Minor Prophets are much shorter. See the chart of the Kings for the chronology of the prophets (page 23).

Message and Style: The Prophets spoke God's word to the people and often to the Kings. They were primarily concerned with 1) Infidelity to God, 2) Injustice of God's people to each other (especially against the poor), and 3) Enemies of God's people. Many of the prophets record warnings to the kings prior to the destruction of Israel or of Judah, and most of the prophetic writing is in the form of Hebrew poetry. There are a couple of books that feel different from this formula. Jonah is mostly narrative, rather than prophetic oracles. Daniel is half narrative and half apocalyptic visions and predictions. His message is about God's sovereignty, however, spoken against pagan kings. Nonetheless, Jewish Scriptures place Daniel among the writings (wisdom literature?) rather than among the prophets. Some books or passages are less specific to a time and place (such as Joel), yet they still contain a message for God's people.

Major Prophets: Isaiah, Jeremiah, Ezekiel and Daniel

These longer works are primarily concerned with the Exile and restoration. Isaiah preaches near the time of the destruction of Israel, and later in the book deals with national restoration. Jeremiah is a prophet at the time of the destruction of Jerusalem, and Ezekiel preaches to the exiles in Babylon. Daniel (more narrative than prophecy in literary form) is set in Babylon as well, though more concerned with living faithfully among pagans than with restoration of Israel.

Isaiah

Isaiah preached against the corruption in Jerusalem at the time that the northern kingdom of Israel was destroyed by Assyria. Isaiah begins with a dramatic vision of the throne room of God, where God calls Isaiah to be a prophet to the people. Isaiah's ultimate vision is for a world blessed by God through the reign of his anointed—his "messiah." The nations stream to the mountain of the LORD, and the vision of "the peaceable kingdom" is described—the lion laying down with the lamb… Isaiah is the source of a lot of messianic prophecy valued by Christians, including that a virgin shall conceive and bear a son called Immanuel (God with us).

Isaiah 40-66: In chapter 40, the mood shifts from judgments against the people and their enemies, toward the restoration of their relationship with God, and their restoration as a nation. This shift (and the language that seems to treat the exile in the past tense), has led some scholars to suggest a different author (or authors) for this section of the book (e.g. "Second Isaiah"). However, there is a great deal of unity in the book, and the second section is highly dependant on the first, especially as it elaborates on the messianic theme. Chapter 40 is well known as the bright opening to this theme of comfort: "Comfort ye, my people!" Chapters 49-57 describe what is called the "suffering servant." These passages are often quoted by New Testament authors since they richly describe the suffering endured by Jesus. In chapters 58-66, the view turns to a final restoration of all things.

Jeremiah

Jeremiah is called as a young man to speak the word of the Lord to the last kings in Jerusalem. Jeremiah decries the people's infidelity to God and their injustice to each other. He warns that God will use Babylon as an instrument of judgment. Jeremiah expresses more than other prophets the anguish of speaking judgment to a people who merely persecute him for "bad news." The kings imprison him and destroy his writings. But Jeremiah rewrites his messages, and stays in Jerusalem, continuing his prophetic ministry. He calls on the king to submit to Babylon (because of the King's oath to God that he would be loyal to Babylon). But the King rebels, and Babylon destroys Jerusalem and the temple and exiles the people. Jeremiah is taken to Egypt, where he continues his denouncements of the people and of their enemies as well.

Ezekiel

Ezekiel prophecies to the exiles in Babylon. His message is distinctive for the wild visions and unusual prophetic acts involved. He brings words of judgment for the people and for the Gentile nations. He also brings words of hope that God will restore his chosen people. Ezekiel sees a vision of wheels lifting up the throne of God from the temple, as "the glory of the Lord" leaves the temple, making it vulnerable to destruction. Later, the "glory of the Lord" returns, making way for the restoration of God's people. Famously, Ezekiel sees a vision of a valley full of dry bones brought back to life by the spirit of God. It is a vision of God restoring the people despite their sin, combined with a vision of resurrection.

Daniel

Daniel is set in Babylon, during the exile and reign of Nebuchadnezzar and Persian kings that followed. Some interpreters (skeptics, especially) claim that Daniel was written centuries later (watch for bias either way in your Bible footnotes). Some traditional lists classify Daniel among the Writings (wisdom literature) due to its different subject matter and narrative form.

Daniel and three friends become courtiers in Babylon. They are shown to be healthy, even though they eat only kosher foods. They remain faithful to God against laws that call them to worship idols. God saves them (the three friends are not harmed by the fiery furnace, and Daniel is not harmed when thrown into the Lion's den). Daniel successfully interprets the king's dreams and the mysterious "writing on the wall" that appears during a royal feast. The message Daniel shares is one of judgment, faithfulness and the sovereignty of God over all kings.

The second half of Daniel has apocalyptic visions—wild visions of enemies of God and their eventual downfall. They include predictions of kingdoms that will rise and fall, especially one who sets up an "abomination to the Lord." Traditionally, these four kingdoms are Babylon, Persia, Greece and Rome. Skeptics (who discount predictive prophecy), think that these four are Babylon, Media, Persia and Greece. Daniel foretells the coming of one who will restore God's people, called "the son of man," a title Jesus uses for himself.

The Minor Prophets: "The Book of the Twelve"

Hosea

Hosea preached against Israel seventy years before its destruction, challenging their infidelity to God. Hosea uses a theme of being married to an unfaithful wife, yet seeking after her return. This is a sign of God's covenant with unfaithful Israel, yet still seeking Israel's return to him.

Joel
Date and place unknown. Joel issues God's call for the people to repent of their sins, proclaiming the "great day of the Lord, with judgment against the sinner and justice for the suffering. Joel offers a vision of a renewed people, where God's spirit will be poured out on all people (invoked by the Apostles at Pentecost, when the Holy Spirit came upon them).

Amos
Around the same time and place as Hosea (earlier in Israel), Amos challenged the leaders and rich in Israel for their oppression of the poor. Amos declares that God does not care for their sacrifices while this injustice continues, in violation of their covenant with God. "Let justice flow down like water, and righteousness like a mighty stream."

Obadiah
This one-chapter book denounces the kingdom of Edom for not defending Judah against its enemies (near the time of the destruction of Jerusalem), and looks ahead to restoration.

Jonah
Narrative (with a psalm of Jonah's prayer). The time period is not specified. God sends Jonah to preach against the Assyrian capital of Nineveh. Jonah tries to flee this call in a sailing ship. He is thrown overboard and swallowed by a fish. God delivers him to the shore and renews his call to Jonah, who then goes to Nineveh and proclaims its downfall. But Nineveh repents and (much to Jonah's anger) God does not destroy the city. A unique statement of God's care for his enemies.

Micah
Micah is a contemporary of Isaiah, prophesying in Judah. He proclaims doom and hope for Judah, using the downfall of the northern kingdom of Israel as an example. He echoes Amos in his denouncement of Israel's empty sacrifices offered while continuing to oppress the poor. Instead, "Do justice, love mercy, walk humbly with your God."

Nahum
Nahum prophesied in Judah, after the fall of Israel in the north. Nahum proclaims judgment and doom for Nineveh, the capital city of the victorious Assyrian Empire. Nineveh fell in 622 BC.

Habakkuk
The Prophet cries out in despair to God after the destruction of Jerusalem: "How long, O Lord", how long?" God answers "Write the vision…" and calls him to stay faithful for God's appointed time of restoration.

Zephaniah:
Against Judah's infidelity and against the Gentile nations, proclaiming the "day of the Lord" for judgment, and the renewal of the remnant. Near the time of the destruction of Jerusalem.

Haggai:
During the return after the exile in Babylon. Haggai prophesies of the rebuilding of the temple and the restoration of the people.

Zechariah:
During the return from exile in Babylon. Zechariah retells apocalyptic visions (wild with symbolism, similar to Revelation) of the restoration of God's people under the messiah.

Malachi:
After the rebuilding of the temple. Malachi rebukes the people for their unfaithfulness, calls them to repentance, and looks ahead to when God will come to purify his people on "The day of the Lord." Then they will offer sacrifices acceptable to God.

The Apocryphal or Deutero-canonical Books

In some Bible translations, there is a section in between the Old Testament and the New Testament commonly called the Apocrypha. Most Protestants do not recognize the Apocrypha as part of the Bible, while Roman Catholics and Eastern Orthodox do, integrating these books into the Old Testament in their Bibles (and sometimes calling these "Deutero-canonical" books, meaning "second canon" books). Some protestants (Anglicans, for instance) regard the Apocrypha as useful for teaching and read from it in the church, despite its secondary status.

Where did they come from? By the time of Jesus, the most common "Bible" for Jews was a translation into Greek called "**the Septuagint**" (~130 BC). This was also the primary Bible used by Jesus and his Disciples and the primary text of the Old Testament for the early church. When Jewish Rabbis established the official Hebrew text of their scriptures after the time of Christ (as early as 100 AD), several books found in the Septuagint were not included in the Hebrew Bible. The church took note of this difference between the Greek and Hebrew texts from time to time.

Protestant challenge: At the Protestant Reformation, many reformers noticed the lack of universal acceptance of these books, and that New Testament writers did not quote from them (as they had quoted from all the other books of the Old Testament). The reformers claimed, therefore, that these books are not the authoritative "Word of God" or part of the canon of scripture. Thus, they called these books "apocryphal," implying less authority. Unlike the original King James Version, many translations of the Bible do not include the Apocrypha (the NIV most notably).

Canonical acceptance: For centuries, however, these books were read along side other Old Testament books from Latin and Greek Bibles and in the English King James Version. In response to the Protestants, the Roman Catholic Church declared most of the books to be canonical (at the Council of Trent in 1546). Most Eastern Orthodox churches, in their own response to the Reformation, generally see these books as canonical, (including a few books from the Septuagint that Rome did not include).

The Apocrypha is mostly Wisdom literature (narrative and proverbs), with some History (Maccabees), Prophecy (Baruch) and Poetry. Included are additions that expand the books of Esther and Daniel in the Greek text.

Book-by-book Overviews

Tobit: God heals faithful Tobit and Sarah (exiles from Israel in the Assyrian Empire) with the guidance of the angel Raphael. Sarah marries Tobit's son Tobias. 15 chapters.

Judith: A mighty empire makes war on many nations, threatening a Judean town where Judith lives (chapters 1-7). Judith challenges the townspeople for their fear of these Gentiles. She infiltrates the army, kills its commander, and initiates an attack that sends them fleeing (8-16).

Additions to Esther: The Greek text of Esther is longer than the Hebrew text. The additions include Mordecai's dream, Haman's edict, prayers of Mordecai and Esther, Esther before the king, Mordecai's version of the royal edict, and an interpretation of Mordecai's dream. These Greek additions add more theological dimension to the original Hebrew story.

Wisdom: (or "The Wisdom of Solomon"): Poetry in the Hebrew style that praises wisdom.
- 1 - 6: Exhortation to Justice
- 6 - 10: In praise of Wisdom
- 11-19: Israel's heroes, and God's justice against idols

Ecclesiasticus (also called "Sirach" or "the Wisdom of Jesus, son of Sirach"): Wisdom proverbs in 51 chapters.

Baruch A prose prayer for mercy, followed by prophetic words of comfort and restoration (in poetry form). 5 chapters. Baruch was the scribe of Jeremiah.

Letter of Jeremiah (chapter 6 of Baruch in some Bibles): a prose statement against idols.

Additions to Daniel: The Greek version of Daniel in the Septuagint includes extra material not found in the Hebrew canon (or Protestant Bibles). These additions include:
- **Song of the Three Jews** (and the **Prayer of Azariah**): a prayer and songs of praise from the three men in the fiery furnace (inserted after Daniel 3:23).
- **Susanna:** chapter 13 in the Greek version of Daniel. Wicked elders try to rape a godly woman, Susanna. She cries out for help, so they falsely accuse her of adultery. Daniel (a young man in this story), prompted by God, proves their guilt and her innocence.
- **Bel and the Dragon:** chapter 14 in the Greek Daniel. Daniel destroys the idol Bel by uncovering lies of its priests. Daniel kills a living beast that the people worshipped (the dragon). When its worshippers rebel, Daniel is cast into the lion's den, but survives by God's providence.

1 and 2 Maccabees: each are parallel accounts of the history around the Jewish revolt against Seleucid (Greek) ruler Antiochus Epiphanes in 167 BC. The revolt was led by Judas Maccabeus, and led to a century of Jewish independence (the "Hasmonean" period), before Rome took power in 63 BC. This is an important history for the time in between the return from exile and the time of Jesus in the first century.

Though not recognized as canonical by the Roman Catholic Church, the following books have some recognition by Eastern Orthodox churches:

1 Esdras: Known in the Russian Bible as 2 Esdras, and in the Douay Bible as 3 Esdras, this book is a retelling of parts of Chronicles, Ezra, and Nehemiah. It begins with King Josiah, continues through the destruction of Jerusalem, and runs through the exile and return.

Prayer of Manasseh: Recognized by the Greek Orthodox Church (but not by the Russian Orthodox Church), this is a short prayer of repentance acknowledging God's mercy. Attributed to King Manasseh after the exile (see 2 Chronicles 33:10-17).

Psalm 151: a brief psalm included in the Septuagint about David, chosen by God and victorious over Goliath. This psalm was also found among the psalms of the Dead Sea Scrolls.

3 Maccabees: Having nothing to do with the Maccabees, this book tells of Egyptian Jews under Ptolemy IV Philopator (221-203 BC). They are persecuted by Ptolemy, but defended by God. This book has mixed status among the Orthodox churches.

2 Esdras: Not appearing in Greek Bibles, but included in Slavonic Bibles of the Russian Orthodox Church (known as 3 Esdras), this is an apocalyptic book (wild visions and signs of God's justice despite the forces of evil). Set in the voice of Ezra, scholars date this book to the first century AD, and relate its concern to the Roman Empire.

The New Testament: The Accounts of the Gospel of Jesus Christ

Outlines: The Accounts of the Gospel

The Gospel According to Matthew
- 1 - 2: Introduction: Origin and infancy of Jesus
- 3 - 7: Part One: Proclaiming the Kingdom (Baptism, temptation, ministry, sermons)
- 8 - 10: Part Two: Ministry and mission in Galilee
- 11 - 13: Part Three: Questioning and opposition to Jesus; parables
- 13 - 18: Part Four: Jesus' identity as the Messiah, Peter's confession, sermons
- 19 - 25: Part Five: Journey to Jerusalem and his ministry there, talk of the end times
- 26 - 28: Suffering, death and resurrection

The Gospel According to Mark
- 1:1-8:26: Part One: Ministry of healing and preaching in Galilee
  - 1:1-3:6: Introduction by John the Baptist, controversy at Capernaum
  - 3:7-6:6: Choosing the Twelve, parables, relatives at Nazareth
  - 6:7-8:26: Sending the Twelve, miracles (including feeding the 5,000) and controversy
- 8:27-16:20: Part Two: to Jerusalem, suffering, death and resurrection
  - 8:27-ch10: Peter's confession, predictions of suffering, transfiguration, teaching
  - 11 - 13: Ministry in Jerusalem: entry, temple actions, discourse on the end times
  - 14 - 15: Anointing, Last Supper, suffering, crucifixion, burial, empty tomb
  - 16: Resurrection appearances and commission

The Gospel According to Luke
- 1 - 9: Part One: Origins of Jesus, and his ministry
  - 1 - 2: Prologue, annunciations, infancy and boyhood of Jesus
  - 3 - 4:13: John the Baptist, Jesus' Baptism and temptation
  - 4:14-9:50: Ministry in Galilee, disciples, sermons, parables, Peter's confession
- 9 - 24: Part Two: To Jerusalem, suffering, death and resurrection
  - 9:51-19:27: Journey to Jerusalem: teaching, healing, exorcism, parables, warnings
  - 19:28-ch21: Ministry in Jerusalem: Entry, cleansing of the temple and teaching
  - 22 - 23: Last Supper, suffering, death and burial
  - 24: Resurrection appearances in the Jerusalem area, ascension

The Gospel According to John:
- 1:1-18: Prologue (in the beginning was the Word...)
- 1:19-12:50: Part One: The Book of Signs
  - 1 - 3: Revelation to the disciples, Jerusalem, Nicodemus, John's testimony
  - 4 - 5: The Samaritan woman at the well, healing the official's son, Sabbath healing
  - 6 - 8: The bread of life, living water, light of the world
  - 9 - 10: Healing of the man born blind (and debate), the good shepherd
  - 11: The raising of Lazarus, Jesus is anointed, the triumphal entry into Jerusalem
- 13-21: Part Two: The Book of Glory
  - 13 -17: The Last Supper: meal, foot washing (13), last discourse & promise (14-17)
  - 18 -19: Suffering, crucifixion (18), death and burial (19)
  - 20 -21: Resurrection appearances and gift of the Holy Spirit

These outlines owe much to Raymond E. Brown's excellent "Introduction to the New Testament" (Doubleday, 1997).

Greatest Hits of The Gospel!

The Gospel ("Evangelium") means "Good News." As a matter of style, there is only one "Gospel," but there are four "accounts" of the Gospel. Readings in bold are most familiar.

Origins of Jesus:

From Eternity: **John 1:1-18:** (In the beginning was the Word…and the Word was God…)
An Angel Foretells Jesus' Birth: **Matthew 1:18-25; Luke 1:26-38**
Birth: **Luke 2:1-21** (wise men and infancy: Matthew 2)

Ministry:

John the Baptist: **Matthew 3:1-12,** Mark 1:1-8, **Luke 3:1-20,** John 1:6-28
Baptism of Jesus: **Matthew 3:13-17,** Mark 1:9-11, **Luke 3:21-22,** John 1:29-34?
Wilderness and Temptation: Matthew 4:1-11, Mark 1:12-13, **Luke 4:1-13**
Wedding at Cana: **John 2:1-11**
Call of the Disciples: **Matthew 4:18-22,** Mark 1:16-20, **Luke 5:1-11,** John 1:35-51
"Sermon on the Mount:" **Matthew 5-7,** Luke 5:17-6:49 ("Sermon on the Plain")
Parables: Mark 4:1-34, 12:1-12, **Matthew 13:1-53, and in Chaps 18-25,**
    Luke 8:4-18, 12:13-21, and in chaps 13-18; in John, Jesus often speaks metaphorically
Parable of the Prodigal Son: **Luke 15:11-32**
Parable of the Good Samaritan: **Luke 10:30-37**
Raising of Lazarus: **John 11:1-44**
Encounter with Nicodemus ("born again"): **John 3:1-17**
The Summary of the Law: Mark 12:28-34, **Matthew 22:36-40,** Luke 10:25-28
Feeding of 5,000: Matthew 14:13-21, Mark 6:30-44, Luke 9:10-17, John 6:1-15
Healing of the Blind: Matthew 20:29-34, **Mark 8:22-26, 10:46-52,** Luke 18:35-43, John 9
Walking on Water: Matthew 14:22-33, **Mark 6:45-52,** John 6:16-21
The Confession of Peter: **Matthew 16:13-20,** Mark 8:27-30, Luke 9:18-21
The Transfiguration: Matthew 17:1-9, Mark 9:2-8, Luke 9:28-36

Suffering (his "Passion") and Death:

Triumphal Entry (Palm Sunday): Matthew 21:1-11, Mark 11:1-11, Luke 19:28-40, John 12:12-19
Cleansing of the Temple: Matthew 21:12-17, Mark 11:15-19, Luke 19:45-48, John 2:13-22
Prediction of Jesus' Return in Glory: Matthew 24:29-51, Mark 13:24-37, Luke 21:25-36
Last Supper: Matthew 26:17-29, Mark 14:12-25, **Luke 22:1-38**, John 13-17
Garden of Gethsemane and Arrest: Matthew 26:30-56, Mark 14:26-50, Luke 22:39-54, John 18:1-12
Peter's Denials: Matthew 26:57-75, Mark 14:53-72, **Luke 22:55-62,** John 18…
Trials: Matthew 26:57-75, 27:1-27, Mark 14:53-72, 15:1-15, Luke 22:63-71, 23:1-25,
    John 18:12-27, **18:28-19:16**.
Suffering and Crucifixion: **Matthew 27:28-54,** Mark 15:16-39, Luke 23:26-47, John 19:16-37

Resurrection:

The Empty Tomb: Matthew 28:1-8, Mark 16:1-11, Luke 24:1-12, **John 20:1-18**
The Road to Emmaus: Mark 16:12 (?), **Luke 24:13-34**
The Disciples (and Thomas): Matthew 27:9-10, Mark 16:12-14, Luke 24:34-49, **John 20:19-31**
The Great Catch of Fish: **John 21:1-14** (and 15-25 about Peter)
The Great Commissions: **Matthew 28:16-20,** Mark 16:15, Luke 24:47, Acts 1:8, John 13:31-35
Ascension: Mark 16:19, **Acts 1:1-11**

Overview: The Accounts of the Gospel

The basic story: The New Testament begins with four books whose titles begin "The Gospel According to…" The "gospel" means "good news," for these are four parallel accounts of the Good News of Jesus: of his origins, his life and ministry, his suffering and death, and his resurrection—rising to life again. You can survey the basic story by reading through the descriptions of the "Greatest Hits" on page 41.

First Century Judea and Samaria

The Gospel story starts with Jesus' origins from God, his miraculous birth in Bethlehem (the City of King David), and his growing up in Nazareth, far to the north of Jerusalem near the Sea of Galilee. He is baptized (a ritual washing as a sign of repentance and renewal) by John the Baptist—a prophet and preacher. He then overcomes temptations and begins a ministry of preaching, teaching, healing and other miracles, including deliverance from evil spirits.

Ministry: His basic message is a call to repentance—turning away from sin and back toward God, to prepare to participate in the "Kingdom of God." He emphasizes not just outward righteousness, and not just inner fidelity to God, but also forgiveness and mercy for the sinner, and the promise of eternal life at a resurrection of the dead. He preaches primarily through "parables," instructive stories that often challenge conventional thinking. These parables raise the bar on righteousness to true fidelity. These parables also expand the vision of God's generosity and mercy (in contrast to a petty legalism). Jesus gathers disciples (student-followers), including twelve men who form an inner circle (called the "apostles"). He calls himself "Son of Man" (a Messianic title) and the Son of God, saying that he is one with the Father in heaven.

He is called "Christ" which means 'Messiah," or "anointed one," fulfilling the prophets' promise of Israel's restoration through God's anointed one. Note that kings in Israel were made not by crowning, but rather by being anointed with oil. When his disciples declare him as the Messiah, the Son of God, Jesus then focuses on his journey to a final confrontation in Jerusalem. There, his preaching challenges the Jewish leaders. He gathers his disciples for the Passover meal, relating the bread and wine to his body and blood to be given for them in the sacrifice of his death for the forgiveness of their sins.

Crucifixion and Resurrection: Judas, one of the twelve, betrays him, and Jesus is captured and tried for blasphemy (for calling himself God). The Jewish leaders hand him over to the Roman rulers, who torture him (as was customary) and then execute him by hanging him on a cross (slowly asphyxiating him). The third day after his death, he is seen alive again by his disciples. He later leaves them to go to the Father in heaven (his "ascension"), but he promises them that they will receive the Holy Spirit and that he will return in power. He sends them to share the good news with the world, to preach repentance and make disciples and baptize and teach them.

Jesus' identity: Jesus presents himself as a different kind of Messiah—not a political king who would make war on the Romans, but one who comes to free us from our sins. The Gospel accounts all lay their primary emphasis on Jesus' crucifixion and resurrection more than his preaching. In part, the Evangelists (authors of the Gospels) had to explain the scandal of worshipping a crucified Messiah. More importantly, Jesus' sacrificial death is central to his message and identity. The cross and resurrection have always been central to the life of the Christian proclamation. Christianity is not simply another system of ethics; Christianity is a promise of forgiveness (and reconciliation with God) through the sacrificial nature of Jesus' death, and the promise of resurrection guaranteed by the Son of God who was the first to rise.

Jesus is primarily identified as *Messiah* (servant of God and king of Israel—in this case a renewal of Israel (the kingdom of God) opened to the whole world, and not just to one ethnic group), *Lord* (relating to the address of God as "the LORD"), *Savior* (delivering us from sin and death, providing new life and resurrection), and *Son of God* (one with God whom he calls Father, giving us the promise of adoption as God's children and heirs of eternal life).

The books of the Gospel: Rather than trying to unify the four into one story, the church from its early decades used all four Gospel accounts together, despite minor differences among them (as we might use various newspaper articles retelling the same event). Each book also has its own objectives and audience. Mark may have been read in one piece. Luke probably wrote for a more Gentile audience, Matthew for a more Jewish audience, and John was more philosophical and theological in style and purpose.

Each of the four books was likely touched by more than one hand. We speak of each "evangelist" (the men Matthew, Mark, Luke and John) writing his own account, but in each case there was probably a more complex process of development guided by the Holy Spirit. The final form of each account was likely developed in a process of experience, oral reports, oral tradition, compilation of this tradition, revisions and edits. These accounts of Jesus' life came not from four men only, but more organically from the Christian communities in which they were formed.

The "Synoptic" Accounts: This development can be seen especially in the first three books: Matthew, Mark and Luke. The three share the same chronology of events. Mark is the shortest account, and Matthew and Luke use large portions of Mark verbatim. Matthew and Luke also expand or develop material found more briefly in Mark. Matthew and Luke each have unique material, but they also share identical material that is not in Mark. These factors suggest that Mark is the first, and the literary basis for Matthew and Luke. These similarities provide a title for these three gospels: the "synoptic" gospels, meaning "from the same eyes." John, on the other hand, sets Jesus' experiences in a slightly different chronology, and in John, Jesus' speeches are more abstract and theological.

Audience and Purpose: Matthew writes for a Jewish audience, presenting Jesus (in five cycles—like the five books of Moses) as a great teacher in the model of Moses. Jesus' words and actions are described as "fulfilling what was written…" in the Hebrew scriptures. Luke writes for a more Gentile audience. Luke emphasizes Jesus' concern for the poor and issues of social justice. Mark, on the other hand is fast paced (with terse stories that frequently transition with the word "immediately"). Mark may have its origins as a single speech delivered orally in one hearing, rather than a book used as a source for smaller pieces of the story. John writes to an audience in conflict with Jewish communities. John emphasizes the miraculous signs that persuade the reader that Jesus is the Messiah and Son of God.

The Synoptic Gospels: In crafting their Gospel accounts, Matthew and Luke build upon Mark, on common material not found in Mark (scholars call this material "Q"), and on their own materials. This common viewpoint and chronology gives these three accounts the title "the Synoptic Gospels" meaning "from the same eyes."

The Gospel According to Matthew

See the previous summary of the Gospel story (p. 42). The final form of Matthew was completed ~80-90 AD. Traditionally by Matthew the tax collector (one of the Twelve), Matthew was edited by a Greek and Aramaic speaker. Matthew is known for its presentation to a Jewish audience. Jesus speaks of the "Kingdom of Heaven" rather than "Kingdom of God." Jesus' actions are constantly measured as "fulfillment of what was written [in the Hebrew scriptures]." Jesus is presented as a great teacher on the mountain, like Moses, and the book can be grouped into five sections, like the five books of the Torah (see p.14). Building on the outline on page 40, the expanded outline below shows how each section concludes with a sermon. The pivot point in the action is again Peter's confession: "You are the Messiah, the son of the living God."

Matthew 1-2: Introduction: Origin and infancy of Jesus
Matthew 3-7: Part One: Proclamation of the Kingdom of Heaven
    3-4: John the Baptist, temptation, Galilean ministry
    5-7: Sermon on the Mount
Matthew 8 – 10: Part Two: Ministry and mission in Galilee
    8-9: Narrative and dialogue: Nine miracles: healings, calming a storm, exorcism
    10: Mission Sermon
Matthew 11 - 13:52: Part Three: Questioning and opposition to Jesus
    11-12: Jesus and John the Baptist, woes on disbelievers, Sabbath controversies
    13:1-52: Sermon in parables
Matthew 13:53 – ch.18: Part Four: Jesus' identity as the Messiah; forming his church
    13:53-16:12: Rejection at Nazareth and by Pharisees; feeding 5,000 and 4,000
    16:13-ch.17: Peter's confession, passion prediction, transfiguration
    18: Sermon on the church
Matthew 19 - 25: Part Five: Journey to Jerusalem and his ministry there
    19 - 23: Teaching, judgment parables, entry to Jerusalem, cleansing temple
    24 - 25: Sermon on the end times
Matthew 26 - 28: Passion, death and resurrection
    26:1-29: Conspiracy, Last Supper
    26:30-27:56: Arrest, trials, crucifixion, death
    27:57-28:20: Burial, opening of tomb, resurrection appearances (and Great Commission)

(This outline is based significantly on the work of Raymond E. Brown's Introduction to the New Testament)

The Gospel According to Mark

See the previous summary of the Gospel story (p. 42). Mark is the shortest and likely oldest account of the Gospel. Known for its fast pace (notice the word "immediately") and its scrappy, confrontational feel, Mark originally may have been delivered orally in one setting. Mark is dated ~60-75 AD, attributed to Mark, traditionally John-Mark mentioned in Acts. Mark's intended audience probably faced persecution and hardship. The pivot point in the Gospel is Peter's confession "You are the Messiah," after which the focus shifts toward the crucifixion.

See the outline of Mark on page 40.

The Gospel According to Luke
See the previous summary of the Gospel story (p. 42). This Gospel account is continued in the Acts of the Apostles by the same writer; the final form completed ~85 AD. Traditionally by Luke the Physician, companion to Paul. Luke builds on Mark and material common to Matthew as well. The pivot point in the Gospel is again Peter's confession "You are the Messiah of God."

Luke writes for a Gentile audience, often translating Aramaic words or phrases (Aramaic was spoken by Jews living in Judea and Galilee) and explaining Jewish customs. Luke has special concern for the poor and oppressed, and is more likely to recall challenges to corrupt authority. Matthew: "Blessed are the poor in spirit." Luke: "Blessed are the poor." Luke uniquely includes the birth narrative, the parable of the Good Samaritan, the Parable of the Prodigal Son, and the resurrection appearance of Jesus on the road to Emmaus. Luke also highlights the activity of the Holy Spirit, from the proclamation of John the Baptist to Jesus' ministry and his promise of the gift of the Holy Spirit to the disciples (continued in Acts of the Apostles). See the outline, p.40.

The Gospel According to John
See the previous summary of the Gospel story on p. 42, and the outline on p. 40. The Gospel According to John is distinctive from the Synoptic Gospel accounts in its language, style, and even its chronology—the sequence of events. John shows three years of ministry, with three trips to Jerusalem, including the "cleansing" of the Temple in the early part of the account. Jesus is portrayed more as a confident martyr rather than as a suffering victim. Jesus speaks in long stately discourses, rich with metaphor and theology. "Seeing" Jesus is important, as is "knowing, abiding in, believing in" Jesus. Themes of light and darkness play a large role. Love, as in mutually abiding in God's love, is a recurring theme.

The Evangelist (the writer/writers of this account) states that this account was "written that you may come to believe that Jesus is the Messiah, the Son of God, and that through believing you may have life in his name" (20:31). This Gospel account is a very literary work, taking the experiences of Jesus and setting them in theological perspective for the writer's stated purpose. This account does not explicitly claim an author, but at the end, the narrator claims that he is "the beloved disciple" who appears in some of the stories, traditionally identified as the apostle John. Three New Testament letters also bear his name and writing style. Scholars sometimes speak about the "Johannine" tradition to reflect the literary tradition of these books.

Tension with "the Jews:" You may notice that there is a strong contrast with the Jews and the synagogue. This seems to indicate that John's community was often persecuted by the synagogue, and saw themselves in stark contrast to the non-Christian Jews. The Greek word used for "Jew" is the same as the word for "Judean," adding to the confusion. We should take care not to read broad-sweeping anti-Jewish sentiment into this Gospel account, as some have done. All the primary Christian actors in the account are Jews themselves, and even some Jewish leaders are accounted favorably (most notably Nicodemus).

Features: John is noted for its description of Jesus' origins in eternity: "In the beginning was the Word and the Word was with God and the Word was God…" John recounts the miracle at the wedding in Cana, the raising of Lazarus from the dead, and Jesus telling Nicodemus to be "born again" (3:1-17). John uniquely recalls Jesus washing his disciples' feet at the last supper, and the resurrection appearance where Jesus helps with a great catch of fish and eats with his disciples.

The New Testament: The Acts of the Apostles

Outline: Acts of the Apostles

Acts 1: Ascension of Jesus and replacement of Judas (ordination)
Acts 2: Pentecost: the coming of the Holy Spirit and institution of the Christian Community
Acts 3 - 8:3 Mission in Jerusalem, preaching, healing and the Holy Spirit
Acts 8:4 - 40: Philip preaches to the outcasts beyond Jerusalem
Acts 9:1 - 15:35: The mission to the Gentiles
    9:1 - 31: The conversion of Saul (Paul)
    9:32 - 11:18: Peter and the Gentiles
    11:19 - 12:25: Persecution of the church
    13:1 - 14:26: Paul's mission to the Gentiles
    14:27 - 15:35: The Council of Jerusalem (what to do about the Gentiles)
Acts 15:36-28:31: Paul's missionary journeys
    15:36 – 18:22: First missionary journey (Antioch, Asia Minor, Greece and return)
    18:23 – 21:14: Second journey (Antioch, Ephesus, Greece, Caesarea)
    21:15 – 26:32: Arrest in Jerusalem and trials
    27:1 - 28:31: Journey to Rome for appeal

Greatest Hits of the Acts of the Apostles!

    Acts 1:1-11: The ascension of Jesus
* **Acts 2:1-18:** The coming of the Holy Spirit at Pentecost
    Acts 3:1-10: Peter heals a crippled beggar
    Acts 4:1-22: Peter and John before the Jewish council
    Acts 6:1-7: Ordination of the first Deacons
    Acts 8:26-40: Philip and the Ethiopian Eunuch
* **Acts 9:1-18:** The Conversion of Saul (Paul)
    Acts 10: Peter's vision, Cornelius and the Gentiles, and their reception of the Holy Spirit
    Acts 15:1-21: The Council at Jerusalem (what to do about the Gentiles)
    Acts 16:16-40: Paul and Silas in Prison
    Acts 17:16-32: Paul preaches to the philosophers of Athens

Overview of Acts of the Apostles

Acts is the sequel to the Gospel According to Luke. This is the story of the birth of the church from the same author/tradition as Luke. Acts is sometimes called "The Gospel of the Holy Spirit" since the Holy Spirit is the prime actor in the narrative. Jesus ascends to heaven, and the eleven apostles choose a replacement for Judas (who betrayed Jesus). Then at the Jewish feast called "Pentecost," the Holy Spirit fills the disciples and they begin to preach in other languages not known to them ("speaking in tongues"). They preach to the visitors from around the empire in their local languages, telling them about Jesus. Many converts are made, and the disciples form a community of mutual care and support, continuing in miraculous ministry of healing, empowered by the Holy Spirit. Jewish authorities arrest some of them, but they continue to preach and teach about Jesus. Deacons are set aside to care for widows and orphans and the poor.

Converts: One deacon, Stephen, preaches about Jesus and challenges the authorities who had him crucified. Stephen is killed for blasphemy by stoning (throwing rocks at his head). More converts are made, including a man named Saul who at first supported the persecution of Christians. Saul sees a vision of Jesus, and he comes to believe and preach the Good News of Jesus. Peter, a leader of the apostles, encounters Gentiles who believe in Jesus and are also filled with the Holy Spirit. This causes some concern in the church: 'Must Gentiles first become Jews in order to be Christians?' A meeting of the leaders in Jerusalem debates the question and ultimately answers no, they can be Christians without becoming Jews first, though there are basic moral standards expected of them.

Paul's Journeys: The narrative then shifts to Saul's missionary journeys, and the narrator writes in the first person: "we" as one of Saul's companions. Saul is a Roman citizen, and his Roman name is Paul; the narrative uses this name starting in chapter 13. Paul is the author of many New Testament letters. Paul and his companions travel throughout Asia Minor and to the Grecian peninsula. They go first to the Jewish synagogue to tell people about Jesus. They then go on to Gentiles with the message, performing miracles as they go. Both groups often give them a hostile response, but Paul starts Christian communities along the way. Paul eventually goes to Jerusalem, where he is arrested. This is not his first arrest, but this time, he appeals to Caesar as is his right as a citizen. Paul gives his "testimony" to various rulers before going by ship to Rome. The narrative ends with Paul in house arrest. Tradition holds that he was executed in Rome around 64 AD.

Throughout Acts, the Holy Spirit directs, speaks, empowers, and heals through the believers. They pray to the Holy Spirit and the Father gives them the Holy Spirit, promised by Jesus. This overlap of identity is consistent with the theology of God as Trinity: One God in three "persons:" Father, Son and Holy Spirit, but all the same one God.

The New Testament: The Letters of Paul

Outlines: The Letters of Paul

Romans: Unity of Gentile Christian and Jewish Christian: Saved by grace, not the law.
- 1-4: Opening; The problem of sin common to Jews and Gentiles; Law does not save
- 5-8: God's salvation for those justified by faith (see ch.8: life in the Spirit; nothing can separate us from the love of God in Christ)
- 9-11: God's promises to Israel
- 12-15: Exhortations to worship, holiness and unity; closing greetings

1 Corinthians: Unity in the body of Christ; spiritual gifts, moral advice
- 1-4: Opening, the problem of factions in the church
- 5-11: Problems of behavior: incest (5), lawsuits (6:1-11), sexual behavior (6:12-20), marriage (7), food sacrificed to idols (8-10:13), the Lord's Supper (10:14-33), and decorum at worship (11)
- 12-14: A variety of Spiritual gifts, but one body of Christ; the greatest is love
- 15-16: The resurrection of Jesus and the Christian; Closing greetings (16)

2 Corinthians: Paul's relationship with them in discipline and love; support of the church
- 1-7: Thanksgivings; Paul's discipline of and love for the Corinthian Christians.
- 8-9: Collection of offerings for the church in Jerusalem
- 10-13: Paul's response to challenges of his apostolic authority (and closing greetings).

Galatians: Paul criticizes them for demanding circumcision; not the law, but grace.
- 1:1-10: Address, then an astonished rebuke in place of the traditional thanksgiving!
- 1:11-2: Paul defends his preaching (credentials, call and relationship to Jerusalem)
- 3-4: Counter-arguments against rival missionaries: Experience of the Spirit, promise to Abraham (made before the Law of Moses), we are heirs to Abraham in Christ, slavery and freedom
- 5-6: Pastoral counsel to the Galatians: Rejecting circumcision, the Fruit of the Spirit, life in the church; Closing (new creation)

Ephesians: Unity in Christ, building up the body, household codes "in Christ"
- 1-3: Greetings; example of what Christ has done for us in humility and unity
- 4: "Therefore:" unity in Christ, building up the body of Christ (the church)
- 5-6:10: Pastoral guidance about morality, mutual submission in the home in Christ
- 6:11-24: The full armor of God; closing greetings

Philippians: Joyful letter about humility, perseverance and joy.
- 1-2: Opening; The Christian life—perseverance, humility and joy; Paul's plans
- 3: The Christian life: confidence in Christ (not works); press on to the goal, hold fast to what you have attained
- 4: Exhortations and thanksgivings: Rejoice in the Lord!

Colossians: Addresses false teachings, the divinity of Christ, vice and virtue.
- 1-2: Opening address, thanks; hymn to Christ, the Lordship of Christ vs. human law
- 3-4: Vices, virtues and household codes; closing greetings

1 Thessalonians: Paul's credentials, hope in the resurrection and second coming.
- 1: Greeting and thanksgiving (especially for their perseverance)
- 2: Paul defends his preaching, demonstrating that he did not serve out of greed
- 3: Paul's relationship with the Thessalonians, including through Timothy
- 4:1-11: Ethics: Sexual purity, brotherly love, respectability and responsible work
- 4:13-5:11: The Second Coming: Be hopeful for those who have died, and be ready
- 5:12-28: Final exhortations (don't put out the Spirit's fire) and final greetings

2 Thessalonians: Corrections about the second coming and how to respond.
- 1: Greeting and thanksgiving (for their vindication in judgment)
- 2:1-12: The "man of lawlessness" to be defeated before the "day of the Lord"
- 2:13-3: Thanksgivings and encouragement; Warning against idleness; final greetings

1 Timothy: Paul addresses correcting false teaching, and leadership issues and standards

2 Timothy: Paul addresses issues of false teaching, and offers encouragement to Timothy

Titus: Ordering and appointment of presbyter/bishops; false teaching; household codes

Philemon: Paul asks Philemon to free his slave Onesimus, welcoming him as a brother

Greatest Hits of Paul's Letters!

Romans 3:22-31: Justification by faith rather than the law
Romans 6:1-14: Dead to sin and alive to Christ
Romans 7:14-25: The struggle of sin, common to all
* **Romans 8:** Life in the Spirit; nothing can separate us from the love of God in Christ

1 Corinthians 3: Against factions: 'Paul planted, Apollos watered, but God gave the growth'
1 Corinthians 7:1-7: mutuality in marriage
* **1 Corinthians 12:** Spiritual gifts and the unity of the Body of Christ
* **1 Corinthians 13:** The greatest of these is love (notice this is primarily about the church!!)

2 Corinthians 4:1-12; 6:3-10: Treasures in clay jars; perseverance

Galatians 3:1-14: You foolish Galatians! Law vs. faith
Galatians 3:26-4:7: No divisions in Christ: heirs of God (to whom we cry "Abba! Father!")
* **Galatians 5:16-26:** The fruit of sin and the fruit of the Spirit

* **Ephesians 4:1-16:** Many gifts to build up the body in the unity of Christ
Ephesians 5:21-6:9: Household relationships *in Christ* (controversial, but there is more mutual submission involved than may be apparent to our 21st century ears)
* **Ephesians 6:10-18:** Put on the full armor of God

* **Philippians 2:1-11:** Make my joy complete: the humility of Christ
Philippians 3:7-14: All else I count as loss; I press on toward the heavenly prize of Christ.
* **Philippians 4:4-9:** Rejoice in the Lord always!

Colossians 1:15-20: Jesus-the image of the invisible God

1 Timothy 3:1-13: Standards for leaders in the church

2 Timothy 4:1-8: Perseverance; I have fought the good fight, run the race, kept the faith

Philemon: Read it several times and wonder what it was like to receive this letter asking you to receive your runaway slave and free him (reading it aloud in front of the church in your house)

Overview: The New Testament Letters of Paul

The Letter form and style: These New Testament books are letters (often called "epistles") written by Paul to churches of various cities that give the letters their names, or in a few cases to individuals (Timothy, Titus and Philemon). The churches are usually ones that Paul helped to establish. These are works of advice, sometimes heavy with theology, sometimes lighter. They are arranged in the Bible from longest to shortest. Each of them has a standard form for a letter of the period: a greeting, a thanksgiving and/or prayer, the body of the letter, and a closing, usually with personal greetings. The letters were likely written by scribes taking dictation. Most were written in the 50s and 60s AD; Timothy and Titus perhaps the latest. Some letters indicate later editing or combining, and some have a difference in style and language. Some interpreters point to this difference in style as an indication of separate authorship (by a disciple of Paul). But the letters claim to be written by Paul, include personal greetings, and their difference in style is either quite subtle or easily explained by a different time, context or audience (to a person rather than to a community). I will assume Pauline authorship in this overview.

Paul: Paul was a convert to Christianity after the resurrection (see Acts 9). Originally an opponent of the Christians, he became an ardent and active evangelist, starting churches throughout the Eastern Roman Empire. He wrote letters to these and other churches, and individuals with whom he worked. Paul's letters are the earliest documentary witness of the Christian faith—written before the completion of the final form of the Gospel accounts. He was frequently imprisoned for his preaching, and likely died in Rome ~64 AD.

Themes: While Paul's letters are often specific with practical advice, there are themes that recur in various forms. The unity of the church is very important to Paul, especially as the early church wrestled with tension between Jewish Christians and Gentile Christians. Paul insisted that Gentile Christians should not be required to be circumcised or hold strictly to Jewish dietary laws. He saw such requirements as placing our good works ahead of Jesus' grace (a free gift). Jew and Gentile alike break the law, so the law cannot save—only Jesus can (see Romans and Galatians). Paul challenges both Jewish Christians and Gentile Christians to see themselves not in light of their old identity, but as new creations in Christ. He counsels them to resolve disputes as brothers and sisters in Christ, not as adversaries. He encourages them that though there may be various gifts and roles in the church, they are all one body in Christ (see 1 Corinthians and Ephesians).

Romans

Romans is the longest of Paul's letters, written ~58 AD from Corinth, to the church in Rome. Paul seems less familiar with this church (whereas he helped to start other churches to whom he wrote). He addresses issues similar to his concerns with the Galatians, but in a far more measured, methodical approach. Paul is concerned with the unity of the church in Rome, resolving tensions between Jewish Christians and Gentile Christians. The Jewish Christians tended to require the Gentile Christians to live according to Jewish standards—including circumcision and Jewish dietary laws.

Paul has two tasks here: to persuade them not to place so high a value on compliance with the law, and to call them to unity together. He argues that all have sinned and fallen short of the glory of God—both Jew and Gentile. Therefore we all need God's forgiveness, and nothing that we do (our futile attempts at good works) can save us—only the grace of God in Jesus Christ can. Does this mean that God's promises to Israel are void? No—God will accomplish his promises to Israel through Jesus Christ, and we are co-heirs of this promise—"both Jew and Greek." Therefore, nothing can separate us from the love of God in Jesus Christ.

1 Corinthians

Paul wrote to the church in Corinth that he helped to start years earlier in this city on the coast of southern Greece. This letter was written in 56 or 57 AD. Paul addresses issues brought to his attention by members of the Corinthian church. While he addresses several practical issues of moral and theological concern, he does so within the lens of unity in Christ. His primary concern is factions in the church. One faction claims loyalty to Paul, in contrast to those with loyalty to Peter or others. Paul finds all this disturbing, and he calls them to greater unity in Christ.

Spiritual gifts: Various factions claim special supernatural gifts of the Holy Spirit, such as speaking in tongues or healing or prophecy. Paul validates all of these gifts as important in the life of the church. But he insists that these gifts are given to build up the whole church in unity of Christ. He uses a metaphor of a human body. There may be many body parts, but they are all essential to the body as a whole—so it is with Christ, for the church is the body of Christ. After addressing these many gifts, Paul writes "Now I will show you a more excellent way." What follows are familiar words about love—often read at wedding ceremonies. But Paul meant them to apply first to relationships in the Christian community. All of these spiritual gifts mean nothing without love for each other. Paul also goes on to reinforce the Christian hope in the resurrection from the dead (as Christ was raised, so shall we be raised). 1 Corinthians is the earliest surviving documentary account of the resurrection of Jesus (chapter 15) and of the Last Supper and the liturgy of Holy Communion in the church.

2 Corinthians:

Paul writes again to the Corinthians, perhaps in 57 AD. Because of some abrupt transitions in the letter, some suggest that this may be a collection of two or more letters. Furthermore, he makes reference to another letter that was not kept or copied by the church. He expresses his love for the Corinthians. He writes of the tension between his fatherly rebuke of them, and his desire to ease their sorrow. He encourages them to be generous in a collection he is raising for the church in Jerusalem, and he reiterates his authority as an apostle, despite his own human weakness. This letter reflects an ongoing correspondence with this church, and Paul's pastoral use of both discipline and mercy for the life of the church. Paul grounds both of these factors in the authority and grace of Jesus (not of Paul himself).

Galatians:

Paul writes from Ephesus or Macedonia between 53 and 57 AD to the church in Galatia (in Asia Minor—modern day Turkey). Galatia is a region, and we are unclear as to which particular city is home to the community that received this letter. As a church that Paul helped to establish, Paul challenges them rather bluntly and passionately (in contrast to the more measured approach in Romans). He criticizes the requirement that some Jewish Christians have made to Gentile Christians—that they must abide by all the ceremonial laws of the Torah, including circumcision.

Paul writes that this emphasis suggests that we are saved by our good works. But we all fail the law. Jesus saves us by his grace—his free gift of salvation. We are justified (a legal term of being found righteous in the eyes of the law) by faith in Christ, not by observing the law. In the free gift of Jesus Christ, we are all saved and united together: Jew and Greek (Gentile), male and female, slave and free: all one in Christ, and co-heirs with him of God's promise. Paul writes about the fruit of sin and the fruit of the Spirit. His message is not one of open license to sin, but rather of the supremacy of God's grace over mere legalism.

Ephesians:

This letter to the church in Ephesus, likely written in the early 60s, stresses their reconciliation and unity in Christ, who in his mercy has made us alive in him. The theme of salvation by faith through grace re-appears, especially to reconcile Jewish Christian and Gentile Christian. Paul encourages them to live in this unity, and to build up the body of Christ by their heartfelt engagement with each other. He stresses the various roles in the church, all of which should be used to "speak the truth in love" to each other and build up the whole body into the full stature of Christ.

He ends with what are called "household codes," including respect for traditional roles for husband and wife. However, there is more of a call to *mutual* submission in this passage than is readily apparent to our 21st century ears, and all of our relationships are set within our mutual submission to one another *in Christ*. For *in Christ*, all our relationships are transformed, and none are used for personal domination (ref. Philemon). He ends with the encouragement to "put on the full armor of God."

Philippians:

Paul writes with passion and beauty to the church in Philippi, a Roman colony that included many retired Roman military personnel. He expresses great joy toward the Philippians, and encourages them in their humility and perseverance (with Jesus as their model). The "hymn to Christ" in chapter 2 is an important record both of Christ's humility and his origins in God: he humbled himself to take flesh and die for us, and through his obedience and death to be exalted again. Paul himself shares in the quest to persevere in faith despite his situation from which he is writing: in prison. Despite his imprisonment, he reminds the Philippians to "rejoice in the Lord always, again I say, rejoice!"

Colossians

Paul writes to the church in Colossae, addressing false teaching and some matters of practical Christian living (including household codes similar to that of Ephesians—see above). Paul's description of the nature of Jesus (his "Christology") is more explicit here: Jesus is the "image of the invisible God," and the authority above all others. From this framework, he builds a contrast for the believer with the surrounding pagan world: to "set your minds on things above, not earthly things."

1 Thessalonians:

This is likely the earliest of Paul's letters in the New Testament, written ~51 AD to the church in Thessalonica (on the southeast coast of Greece) that Paul helped establish. The Thessalonians are weary from the persecutions they face for their faith. Paul assures them of the truth of his message and encourages them to persevere. He also reminds them of the hope of the resurrection and return of Jesus—that those who die in the Lord will be the first to rise when Christ returns. He goes on to advise them on practical matters of the Christian life.

2 Thessalonians:

This letter provides more encouragement but, as a counter-balance to 1 Thessalonians, this letter corrects an over-emphasis on the immediacy of the second coming of Jesus, and an impatience in waiting for this return. Paul writes that there will be more evil and challenge to Christ before the day of his return. So "stand firm, and hold to the teachings we passed on to you."

The Pastoral Letters (1 and 2 Timothy and Titus):
The letters to Timothy and Titus are known as the "Pastoral Epistles." They offer advice on how to lead in the church. They present a more structured approach to leadership than Paul's other letters (leading some to claim authorship by a disciple of Paul). This difference may also arise from the intended audience: an individual (and a leader at that), rather than a community.

1 Timothy:

Paul writes to Timothy, who was his co-worker on missionary journeys. Paul advises Timothy on how to correct false teaching and establish standards for leadership in the church. This is one biblical source for the offices of bishop (overseer), presbyter (elder/priest), and deacons (those who serve). Widows also seem to have an official role in the church. Paul addresses decorum at worship, and instructions for slaves and rich people.

2 Timothy:

Paul writes with great affection to his colleague in ministry. He advises him on dealing with false teachers, but primarily, Paul encourages Timothy to persevere in his faith and ministry, even as Paul has persevered despite his current imprisonment. "I have fought the good fight, run the race, kept the faith."

Titus:

Paul writes to Titus, another missionary colleague leading the church in Crete. He advises Titus on the ordering and appointment of leaders in the church. In this case presbyter and bishop are used somewhat interchangeably for various leadership roles. The church structure had not yet developed the more hierarchical structure of bishop, presbyter/priest and deacon (though it did so by the early 100s AD). Paul also addresses false teaching and includes more advice on family structure and household codes.

Philemon:

This is Paul's shortest letter—about freedom and brotherhood in Christ. Written by Paul from prison in Ephesus or Rome to Philemon (usually pronounced as if it would rhyme with "pie-LEE-mun") and the church in Philemon's house. The person who delivered this letter is Onesimus (usually pronounced "oh-NEE-sih-muss"). Onesimus was Philemon's slave who had run away to Paul (and he may have stolen from Philemon). The penalty for a runaway slave was death. But Paul sent him back to Philemon with this letter, to be read in front of the church that met in Philemon's house. Paul asks Philemon to welcome Onesimus, not as a slave, but as a brother in Christ.

The New Testament: Hebrews and the General Letters

Outlines: Hebrews and the General Letters

Hebrews: A sermon on the sufficiency of Jesus' sacrifice, and perseverance
- 1-7: The superiority of Christ: to angels (1-2), Moses & priests (3-7)
- 8-10: Christ's sacrifice (once for all) is superior to the sacrifices of the law
- 11-13: Perseverance in faith and fidelity; boldness before God

James: Faith in action, temptation, our speech, worldliness, warnings to the rich
- 1: Trials & Temptations
- 2-3:12: Hearing and doing; faith and action (e.g. vs. favoring the rich; the tongue)
- 3:13-4:12: Submitting to God's wisdom vs. selfish "wisdom"
- 4:13-5:6: Warnings to the rich oppressors
- 5:7-20: Patience in suffering; the prayer of faith

1 Peter: Advice of holiness to Christians in a pagan world
- 1: Call to holiness in response to salvation
- 2-3:12: Appropriate behavior for good witness in the pagan world
- 3:13-5: Christian behavior and humility in the face of hostility

2 Peter: Another general letter
- 1: progress in virtue, faithfulness to your calling; the truth of the Gospel
- 2: condemnation of false teachers (quotes Jude)
- 3: patience for the second coming

1 John: Reject false liberal teaching; walk in the love of Christ
- 1-3:10: Walk in the light: the reality of sin and hope of forgiveness
- 3:11-5:21: Love one another as Christ loves us

2 John: Beware of heretical missionaries; test their message

3 John: A personal letter: encouragement and warnings about a problematic leader

Jude: A warning against licentious teaching; preserving "the faith once delivered"

Greatest Hits of Hebrews and the General Letters!

Hebrews 11: Those great witnesses who lived "by faith" for the promise…
* **Hebrews 12:1-13:** Therefore, since we are surrounded by so great a cloud of witnesses…

* **James 1:19-27:** Be doers of the word and not merely hearers
James 2: Faith and faith in action
* **James 3:1-12:** Taming the tongue (or in today's world: email!)

1 Peter 2: 9-10: You are a chosen people, a royal priesthood…

1 John 1:8-2:6: The response to sin: confession and forgiveness
1 John 4:7-21: God's love and ours

Jude 17-25: A call to persevere

Overview: Hebrews and the General Letters

Hebrews:

While the title of this book is "to the Hebrews," it is missing some of the standard letter components. Hebrews seems to be a sermon on the sufficiency of Jesus' sacrifice, and a call to perseverance in faith. Though some in the early church thought that Hebrews was written by Paul, there is no attribution within the book itself, and the style is dramatically different from Paul's works. The first ten chapters compare Jesus' self-sacrifice for our sins, "once for all," to the sacrificial system of the Old Testament that had to be repeated yearly. The last three chapters then appeal to the examples of those who have gone before us in faith, with a call to persevere in faith and approach God with full confidence of our redemption.

The General Letters (also called the "Catholic Letters" or "Catholic Epistles")

These letters address a more general audience, rather than specific communities. Some interpreters challenge the authorship claims of these letters, but the evidence for such theories is far from compelling. Most were attested by other literature by ~100 AD.

James:

Written by James, generally thought to be the same James who is the "brother of the Lord" and a leader in Jerusalem. This is a strongly practical and concrete letter, calling the reader to put faith into action, for "by my works I will show you my faith." Among the actions James encourages is taming of our speech and conversation (his warning about "the tongue"), and standing firm in temptation. He warns the rich for their materialism and their indifference to and oppression of the poor. He calls us to patience in suffering and to praying for each other.

1 Peter:

Peter writes at a time of persecution, encouraging Christians to be hopeful and pursue holiness of life. He advises his readers to respect authority in the public world, the family and in the church. He also advises those in traditional leadership roles to show humility and live as examples rather than "lording over" those they lead.

2 Peter:

With a different style and emphasis from 1 Peter, this letter quotes Jude (see below) in addressing false teachers and encouraging faithfulness and patience as they await Jesus' return.

1 John, 2 John and 3 John:

These three letters are consistent with the style and themes of the Gospel according to John, though more concerned with false teaching within the church. **1 John** responds to an early heresy that taught Jesus had not come in the flesh, but was pure spirit. This early form of Gnosticism allowed licentiousness, teaching that there is no sin and thus permitting sinful behavior. John emphasizes the hope of forgiveness and the call to love one another as Christ loved us. **2 John** gives warnings to test the message of heretical missionaries. **3 John** is a more personal letter, encouraging the reader and warning about a problematic leader in the church.

Jude:

From Jude "the brother of James," which would make him a brother of Jesus, assuming this is "James the brother of our Lord." Jude warns against a false teaching that permits loose standards and sinful behavior. Jude calls the reader to preserve "the faith once delivered to the saints."

The New Testament: The Revelation to John

Outline: Revelation

1: Opening and vision of Christ
2-3: Letters to seven churches of Asia Minor: clean-up, persevere, get ready.

Visions of the struggle:
- 4-5: Vision of the throne room of God; the scroll to be read
- 6-7: Six of the seven seals of the scroll: doom to come, and the saints to be saved.
- 8-11: The seventh seal and seven trumpets: signs of doom and triumph.
- 12-13: A woman giving birth; A great dragon; a great, blasphemous beast.
- 14: The lamb on the throne and the promise for the faithful.
- 15-18: Images of plagues, wrath, the abyss, Babylon falling.

19-22: Victory and new life in the new Jerusalem.

The Greatest Hits of Revelation!

Revelation 2-3: Letters to seven churches (clean-up, persevere, be ready)
Revelation 4: The vision of the throne room of God
Revelation 5: The vision of the lamb who was slain and is victorious (an image of Jesus)
* **Revelation 21:1-7:** The vision of the new Jerusalem

Overview: the Revelation to John

Title: The Greek title of this book is *Apocalypsis*, a word meaning "unveiling" or revelation. Contemporary language now reads the word "apocalypse" as a destructive end of the world precisely because of the content and style of this book. However, this kind of literature was not new. We now use the term "apocalyptic literature" for Zechariah and the second half of Daniel in the Old Testament. This literature presents highly symbolic visions 'unveiling' the unseen reality of a great cosmic struggle between the power of evil and the victorious power of God.

Author: This is especially meaningful to those who are experiencing extended persecution in a world where evil seems to have the upper hand. This revelation comes to John on the island of Patmos. Though there are some echoes from the Gospel according to John and John's letters, many have argued that John of Patmos is not the apostle John.

Overview: The book opens as a letter to seven churches in Asia Minor, with specific messages to each of them (clean up, persevere, get ready). The book then shifts to a series of visions with repeated cycles of unveiling and unfolding signs and symbols, preparing for the doom of the evil that rules in the world. Wild images of beasts and battles and the end of all things fill the bulk of the book. In the midst of the chaos and terror are the faithful that God will preserve, and images of the lamb that was slain (a symbol of Jesus' sacrifice) sitting on the throne of God. At the end of the book, evil is conquered and a new heaven and a new earth come from God out of heaven. The faithful are raised and death and sorrow are no more.

The use of Revelation: Revelation is not a secret book for decoding a timetable that dates Jesus' return (though it is often abused this way). Though it has been used against numerous kings and powers through the centuries, it is far less for a *specific* earthly power and more for the recurring evil powers that challenge and persecute Christ's faithful people. John calls us *always* to be ready and stay faithful, for the evil powers of this world that seem to have the upper hand are and will be defeated by God, and all things will be made new when Jesus returns.

PART III: Resources for Further Learning

Guide to Translations and Published Editions 58
How did the Bible Become the Bible? 60
Analytical Methods 62
Interpretive "World-views" that Influence How We Understand the Bible 64
Reading Strategies (tables of what to read when) 65
Additional Resources (Annotated Bibliographies and References) 74
Glossary 76
Index 82
Map of Ancient Near East .... Inner Front Cover
Map of Ancient Israel and Judah… .... Inner Front Cover
Chart of the Books of the Bible .... Facing Inner Front Cover
Map of New Testament Cities and Regions .... Inner Back Cover
Map of First Century Judea and Samaria .... Inner Back Cover

Guide to Translations and Published Editions of the Bible

Why are there so many different Bibles and which one should I use?

A visit to any library or bookstore will overwhelm you with options for various different kinds of Bibles. Why are they all so different and what makes them different? Which one should you use? Below is an explanation of these differences, and a review of many popular (and some rather unusual) translations and editions of the Bible.

Translations vs. Editions

It may be helpful to draw a distinction between *Translations* and what I would call *Editions* of the Bible. *Translations* are official texts of translations from the original Hebrew and Greek texts, usually prepared by groups of translators. Publishers then package this translation into Editions that add footnotes, introductions, marginal commentary, maps, cross references, life applications, indexes or other resources. These editions are often packaged to appeal to various demographic groups such as teenagers, women, students, children, etc. Thus there are numerous *Editions* of the NIV *Translation* (the *Quest Study Bible*, the *NIV Study Bible*, the *Adventure Bible*, etc.) Note that the footnotes and introductions are not part of the Bible (nor are they the authoritative interpretation), but rather, they are the *opinion* of a commentator. That's why some sets of footnotes disagree with others!

Understanding the Different Translations

The Old Testament was written in Hebrew (with a little Aramaic), and the New Testament was written in Greek. Translation always involves interpretations and strategies for rendering things into English—the choice of words, the crafting of phrases--even separating lines into paragraphs is an interpretive decision. So there are many different English translations. Translation strategies can produce *accurate* renderings, but they may not be smoothly *readable* in English (these are sometimes called more "wooden" translations). Likewise, others may be very readable, but not as accurate in the details.

Thus, if you are encountering a text for the first time, a readable translation makes it much easier to consume. But if you are studying a text and get stuck on a word (e.g. "why does Jesus say "return" in this verse?"), you may want a translation that most accurately renders each word. Some translations, such as the *Living Bible*, and *The Message*, are paraphrases—loose translations that move phrase by phrase and use a lot of contemporary idiom to make it easier to read. These will be the most different from other translations in a Bible Study group.

Below is a quick guide to various translations of the Bible, starting with some of the more popular versions. The assessments below are, of course, my own opinion…

- **KJV:** **King James Version:** The classic and beloved "Authorized Version" first published in 1611 is prized for its beautiful language. It is an accurate translation for the scholarship of its time, but the older forms of English (e.g. using "thee" and "thou") make this often difficult to read, especially for those new to the Bible.
- **RSV:** **Revised Standard Version:** The 1950s successor to the KJV. A good translation, but it keeps "thee" and "thou" for God. Less common since publication of the NRSV.
- *** NRSV:** **New Revised Standard Version:** The 1989 successor to the RSV. It is fairly accurate, and consistent in translating special vocabulary (see the section on special vocabulary

in Part I). However, its emphasis on gender neutrality (avoiding using masculine language and pronouns) sometimes becomes awkward or inaccurate. It also tends always to translate "servant" as "slave" (the word can mean both) in ways that are not always helpful. Mainline Protestant churches tend to use the NRSV in worship. One of the common Editions of the NRSV is the *New Oxford Annotated Edition*.

* **NIV:** **New International Version:** 1980s; from evangelical scholars. One of the most popular translations for Americans. The NIV may be helpful for young readers and those new to the Bible as a good balance between accuracy and readability, though you might not always notice when special vocabulary is being used. Notes in most editions of the NIV tend to take the text at face value, which is often more helpful in Bible study than some of the heavily "critical" approaches used with other translations.
* **ESV:** **English Standard Version:** Revised in 2007, The ESV is an update from Evangelical scholars based on the RSV. Less wooden than the NASB, but more accurate than the NIV, and without some of the clumsy gender translation issues of the NRSV. This translation is growing in popularity.
  NASB: **New American Standard Bible:** Revised in 1995, this is a good, accurate translation, but a bit wooden in readability. Helpful for close word-study.
  NEB: **New English Bible:** 1970, revised in 1989 as the **REB: Revised English Bible.** Generally British English versions; I don't find them as accurate as the RSV/NRSV.

Translations especially for Roman Catholics:

NAB: **New American Bible:** Revised in 2011 from Roman Catholic Scholars. This is a generally accurate translation, though it adopts different habits of vocabulary than most Bibles in the King James tradition (the ones above).
JB: **The Jerusalem Bible** is a Roman Catholic translation from the 1960s. Fairly readable, it is much less used since the publication of the NAB. Distinctive for its use of "Yahweh" for the divine name (rather than "the LORD").
Douay: **The Douay-Rheims** is a Roman Catholic translation from the 16th century, similar to the KJV. The Douay-Rheims was based primarily on the Latin "Vulgate" translation.

Paraphrases:

*"**The Message: The Bible in Contemporary English,**" published in 2002, is a popular paraphrase by Eugene Peterson from the Hebrew and Greek. Many would describe this paraphrase as "casual," verging on slang. Peterson's work is far more scholarly and accurate than Taylor's *The Living Bible*. His purpose is not to replace translations, but rather to help those unfamiliar with the Bible feel the energy and directness of the story. This is an excellent supplement, especially for teenagers.

"**The Living Bible,**" published in 1971, is a paraphrase by Kenneth Taylor (from the American Standard Version of 1901). Popular in the 1970s, this is a readable, but far less accurate translation. Much less used today.

GNB: **Good News Bible** (aka **Good News Translation-GNT** or **Today's English Version-TEV**): a 1960s translation with later revisions; readable but very loose translations—almost paraphrases. Much less used today.
CEV: **Contemporary English Version:** A newer paraphrase from 1995, in very fluid English, but with very loose accuracy.

An outlier:

NWT: **The New World Translation:** a startlingly inaccurate translation from the Jehovah's Witnesses. For instance, subtle changes present Jesus as a separate god... yikes!

How Did the Bible Become the Bible?
The Development of the "Canon of scripture"

How and when were these ancient writings recognized with the authority of the "Word of God?"

The Old Testament:

Jews had chosen the scriptures holy to them before the time of Christ. These are the Old Testament scriptures, written from oral histories, original writings and chronicles, and compilations by the Jewish communities that preserved them.

The Old Testament is an anthology of writings from over many centuries, many relying on older oral and written tradition. There is evidence in the Biblical text that, in some cases, two or more accounts of the same event are included in the narrative, indicating that multiple traditions were both carefully preserved and brought together. One theory suggests two or perhaps four sources for the Torah (the first five books). These strains of tradition are usually titled by the letters J, E, D, and P. One notices J writings by the references to God as "Yahweh" or "The LORD" in most translations (all capital letters). E, on the other hand, refers to God as "God."

Though many texts have early origins, modern scholars focus on the time around the exile as a time when many earlier texts were compiled together (roughly 600 BC). Other prophetic writings followed. Dating *the writing* of these ancient texts is *very* difficult, so take specific claims (even "scholarly" claims) with great caution.

The people of Israel (especially the Jewish people returned after the exile) used all of these texts together as authoritative. By the time of Jesus, the most common "Bible" for Jews was a Jewish translation into Greek called **"The Septuagint"** (completed ~130 BC). Hebrew was no longer a commonly spoken language for Jews (Aramaic was more common in Judea), and the language most common to Mediterranean culture was Greek. The Septuagint contained the Torah, the Prophets and the Writings (and the Apocryphal/Deutero-canonical books). The Septuagint was widely quoted by New Testament authors and the early church.

The New Testament:

The earliest texts of the New Testament are Paul's letters (as early as 51 AD). Though they naturally relied on oral tradition and earlier written works, the final form of the Gospel accounts appeared later (with the Gospel according to John as the latest to settle into its final form). All of the New Testament writings date to before 100AD (Revelation being perhaps the latest).

The New Testament Gospel accounts and letters were considered authoritative in the church and circulated all over the Roman Empire. We see some teachers as early as 90 AD quoting these writings as authoritative support for their teaching. By 100 AD prominent teachers provided lists of which books were authoritative. These are the same books that form the bulk of the New Testament.

Some of these texts, especially the Gospel accounts, show some editing and cross-influence (Matthew and Luke seem to rely on Mark quite a bit), and each text reflects the context of particular communities facing particular issues. But these books were widely used and authoritative throughout the church early on. The question of "official" designation of the New Testament books arose later in order to clarify some theological confusion.

Setting the standard by using the older books
~150 AD, some teachers began to teach theology quite different from traditional Christian theology, for instance speaking *against* the whole Old Testament, saying that the God of the Old Testament was a separate god from the God of the New Testament, and denying that Jesus was human at all, but only a spirit (physical = bad, spirit = good). This line of thought known as "Gnosticism" was very different from the Christian witness and needed a clear response from the rest of the church. A significant part of the response was to determine what had always been openly taught and believed and used by the church everywhere (what was "catholic"), what had apostolic authority, and what had been important for the church's teaching to preserve in historic centers of the church. This effort brought clarity to which writings met these criteria all over the church (and included the Old Testament).

Much of the existing New Testament was used widely as a complete collection fairly early on—perhaps ~AD 130 or earlier, by evidence from other writings. In the many decades that followed, the finer points of what was considered authoritative (there were some questions on a couple of the letters in some quarters) were refined between centers of the church in the east and west of the Roman Empire. A Council of bishops in the late 300s AD affirmed the authority of the current New Testament collection, but the decision was based on substantial precedent. Broad recognition of this collection was uniform by 400 AD. We call this official list the "canon of scripture."

The Apocrypha or Deutero-canonical books: (see pages 38-39)

In some Bible translations, there is a section in between the Old Testament and the New Testament commonly called the Apocrypha. Most Protestants do not recognize the Apocrypha as part of the Bible, while Roman Catholics and Eastern Orthodox do, integrating these books into the Old Testament in their Bibles (and sometimes calling them "Deutero-canonical" books, meaning "second canon" books). Some protestants (Anglicans, for instance) regard the Apocrypha as useful for teaching and read from it in the church, despite its secondary status.

Where did they come from? The Septuagint is the pre-Christian Jewish translation of Jewish scriptures into Greek completed ~130 BC. This was the primary Bible used by Jesus and his Disciples and the primary text of the Old Testament for the early church. When Jewish Rabbis established the official Hebrew text of their scriptures after the time of Christ (as early as 100 AD), several books found in the Septuagint were not included in the Hebrew canon. The church took note of this difference between the Greek text and the Hebrew text from time to time.

Protestant challenge: At the Protestant Reformation, many reformers were concerned about the lack of universal acceptance of these books, and they noticed that New Testament writers did not quote from them as they had quoted from all the other books of the Old Testament. The reformers claimed, therefore, that these books are not the authoritative "Word of God" or part of the canon of scripture. Thus, they call these books "apocryphal," implying less authority. Many translations of the Bible do not include the Apocrypha (the NIV most notably).

Canonical acceptance: For centuries, however, these books were read along side other Old Testament books from Latin and Greek Bibles. In response to the Protestants, the Roman Catholic Church sought to make a definitive statement about these books, and declared most of them to be canonical at the Council of Trent in 1546. Most Eastern Orthodox churches also see these books canonical, but they included other books that had been part of the Septuagint (including a few that Rome did not include).

Analytical Methods
What tools can we use to better understand the Bible?

The study of the Bible has been enriched by various methods of analyzing and understanding the text. **These are tools and perspectives on the task known as "exegesis."** Exegesis means getting the meaning *from* the text—answering the question of what the text meant to those who wrote and heard it in its present form. "Eisegesis," on the other hand, is the opposite: taking meaning of our own, and putting it *into* the text. Eisegesis is where someone works to interpret the Bible so that his or her own opinion could be found (such as slaveholders looking for a positive message about slavery, even in passages that condemn it). Good exegesis, however, tries to avoid such mistakes, and tries to hear what the text itself says.

Some of these methods are very helpful, and all of them have been abused to warp the meaning of scripture. So be equipped, but be careful in how you use these tools.

Textual Criticism: Used especially for the New Testament to evaluate the precise wording of the original document when presented with a number of ancient copies of the same text. Sometimes these copies differ slightly on a word here or there, so Textual Criticism helps to point to the most likely form of the original wording.

Historical/Hermeneutical: This kind of analysis looks at the historical setting so that the text might be better understood—that is, to ask how the original listeners and readers of these texts would have understood them. For instance "The cat had no bread" might mean one thing in a pet shop, but another thing in a Harlem Jazz club.

Source Criticism: Attempting to determine and describe the writer or writers (sources) of a given passage. One of the original issues for modernists, this analysis of the Bible noticed that certain Biblical passages use certain vocabulary, while other passages within the same book use different vocabulary. A theory might then be suggested that the two passages came from different writers or different oral traditions (different sources) which were later combined together. Genesis gets the most attention here, where one can find parallel versions of the same story. Modernists split the two apart and show their differences. Canonical criticism, however (see below) notices that someone put them together, and that some of the texts don't always strictly hold to the "rules" of modernist categories. Canonical criticism, therefore, asks what the final form meant to those who put these traditions together, and how the different perspectives complement each other.

Form Criticism: This kind of analysis finds help in understanding a passage by noticing its literary form or genre: is it poetry, history, preaching, parable, narrative, allegory, etc. Genre can give clues to intent of how a piece of writing might be used. Poetry that suggests "God is a rock" is more likely to be allegorical while "crucified under Pontius Pilate" would be taken as a clear historical reference rather than allegory. This can be abused by our own bias. For instance, someone wanting to avoid the possibility that God might really be involved in history might take any account of a supernatural event and label it "fable" to avoid the plain meaning of the text.

Narrative and Rhetorical Criticism: These approaches look for the way language is used, especially in the context of the time in which the text was written.

Sociological: This approach looks for the interplay between communities, their social and political context, and the way this influences and is influenced by language, beliefs and theology.

Advocacy/Liberation/Feminist/Womanist: These approaches notice the emphasis in many Biblical writings on oppression of the poor, and the problem of how power influences religion and religious teaching. This approach tends to focus almost exclusively on the question of what value the text might have (or not have) in liberating any of a number of social groups (poor, minorities, women, black women, third world peoples, etc.). At its best, this approach challenges the assumptions of readers from the majority. At its worst, this approach asks only "what does this say about what I feel is important?" rather than asking "what does this say to me, that perhaps *should* be important?"

History of Interpretation: this method looks at how texts have been interpreted through the 2000 years of Christian history. This tool finds insights by considering the text from contexts and viewpoints different from our own.

Canonical Criticism: This approach (see "source criticism" above) uses these critical methods while recognizing the theological importance of the text and its place within the Bible as a whole. Thus, instead of studying ancient religion (source and historical criticism), or finding a way to express our own views with religious language (advocacy), we might approach the Bible as an integrated theological text, listening for the voice of a living God.

So What?!

Rarely does someone sit down to read the Bible trying to do all these things at the same time, or even some of these things, unless that person does it for a living. Even then, most theologians simply have these tools in the background as they just read the Bible. You don't have to be an expert in this stuff to do so—most of these are tools of recent history. Ideally, these are just perspectives that enhance this task as one digs deeper into the text.

How should one read the Bible? Prayerfully—listening for the voice of the living God, and in community with others who are doing the same (and those from Christian history who have done the same), listening for the voice of the Holy Spirit speaking through them as well.

See the next page regarding "interpretive worldviews"

Interpretive World-Views that Influence How We Understand the Bible

"Pre-critical:" So-called by the modernists of the enlightenment age who developed new methods of literary analysis, the term "pre-critical" casts all earlier Biblical analysis (some of it rather intensely analytical) into a rather wide and disrespected basket. History of Interpretation shows that this assumption doesn't hold. But the category stuck, so if you hear it, this is what it means.

Modernism: Describes the rise of the renaissance, and the enlightenment ideas of pure reason being seen as the road to truth. Modernism relied heavily on the scientific method of testable, repeatable truths. Biblical criticism tended to propose alternatives to any supernatural references in the Bible, bringing the Bible more into line with their Deist view of a God who made everything, but is never involved in the affairs of creation. This gave rise to religious attitudes that denied the divinity of Christ, preferring to cast Jesus as a great teacher. This fit a cultural trend that held a completely optimistic view of human nature and the ability of humanity to build for itself the Kingdom of God through social and political reform.

This view survives, but its foundations and zeal were shattered by the reality of human evil displayed in WWI and WWII. Theologians in the middle 20th century responded with "Neo-orthodoxy" that re-captured the theological foundations of Christianity, while making use of some of the analytical insights found by the modernists (see below).

Post-Modernism: The scientific skepticism of the spiritual, and the modernist quest for certainty began to give way to a view more open to mystery, claiming that truth cannot be determined. Taken further, there is no truth, or truth is relative, or there are many "truths." One hears such phrases as "that's truth for you, but not truth for me—but they are both true." Post-modernism finds and presents truth in stories or histories that convey meaning metaphorically, but they allow the content of the story itself to be extraneous. At its best, Post-modernism revives a theological approach to the Bible vs. an archeological approach, and is comfortable with mystery and our inability to answer all the questions about God. At its worst, Post-modernism teaches that the Bible is whatever we make it to be, even to Orwellian extremes of double-speak, where one can teach the exact opposite of a Biblical passage and call such teaching Biblical.

Critical Realism: There is no consensus world view replacing Post-modernism, though some have suggested alternatives to both modern and post-modern thinking, including Critical Realism. Critical Realism notes the excesses of post-modernism, and concedes that truth can be known, at least to a useful extent, or otherwise our language and education would be meaningless. However, there is still mystery that science and reason may not be able to adequately describe. Thus while the modernist skeptic sees Genesis as a quaint story meaningless for today, and while the fundamentalist regards Genesis as a science text (in itself, a modernist approach), and while the post-modernist makes out of Genesis whatever one wishes to hear, a critical realist would listen for the theological truths that Genesis teaches. Critical realism is one label for a growing trend among many thinkers, scholars and theologians who reject modernism's stark absence of spirituality while also rejecting post-modernism's avoidance of truth claims. We can make claims about God and humanity and the world, and those claims aught not be limited to only what the scientific method demonstrates. God and God's activity in the world is real, AND we can still learn a lot by asking tough questions.

Reading Strategies

Find below the details of several strategies for starting to read the Bible. These strategies are listed in order of smaller samples to strategies for reading the whole Bible.

- 20 Bible Basics: a starter sampler of twenty key passages 65
- Greatest Hits: 46 or 130 brief passages (5-10 minutes each) 66
- An introduction with five whole books of the Bible: 71
- Three two-week courses, a chapter a day: 71
- Reading Most of the Bible (abridging the Old Testament) 72
- Reading all of the Bible over one to three years 73

20 Bible Basics: a starter sampler of twenty key passages:

These are twenty familiar or important passages that help to frame the basic narrative of the Bible. Start with these, then add more of the "Greatest Hits" from the other strategies. With the exception of the first and 11th selections, all are brief (less than 10 minutes to read), so the list can be completed in a matter of days. Take time to pray before and after you read these passages and save time to ponder the meaning and significance of the text.

1. **Genesis 1-3:** Creation and the Fall
2. **Genesis 12:1-7:** The Call of Abraham
3. **Exodus 3:1-15:** Moses, God and the burning bush
4. **Exodus 20:1-20:** The Ten Commandments
5. **1 Samuel 17:** David and Goliath
6. **Amos 5:21-24:** A prophet speaks for justice
7. **Jeremiah 39:1-10:** Jerusalem is destroyed and exiled
8. **Isaiah 53:** The suffering servant
9. **Ezekiel 37:1-14:** The valley of dry bones
10. **Matthew 3:13-17:** Baptism of Jesus
11. **Matthew 5-7:** The Sermon on the Mount
12. **Luke 15:11-32:** Parable of the Prodigal Son
13. **Luke 22:1-38:** The Last Supper
14. **Matthew 27:28-54:** Suffering and crucifixion
15. **John 20:19-31:** Resurrection
16. **Acts 2:1-18:** Pentecost
17. **Acts 9:1-18:** The conversion of Paul
18. **1 Corinthians 12:** The body of Christ
19. **Galatians 5:16-26:** The fruit of the Spirit
20. **Revelation 21:** The vision of a new heaven and a new earth

Bible Reading Strategy: 46 or 130 Greatest Hits (over one or two months)

These are 130 gems from the Bible, selected based on their importance and as a sampling of the sections they represent. Read two each day, (~15 minutes), five days a week for three months. Or make your own schedule. Each passage takes around five minutes to read. Or read two of the selected 46 passages marked with * each day for a month.

The Old Testament

The Torah:

1. ***Genesis 1 and 2:*** Creation; God makes man and woman in his image
2. ***Genesis 3:*** The man and woman sin ("The Fall")
3. **Genesis 6:5-9:17:** Noah and the flood, and God's covenant
4. **Genesis 12:1-7:** The Call of Abram (See the whole Abraham saga, Genesis 12-25)
5. **Genesis 22:1-18:** The "sacrifice" of Isaac
6. ***Genesis 32:22-32:*** Jacob wrestles with God and becomes "Israel"
   See the whole Joseph saga, Genesis 37-50.
7. ***Exodus 3:1-15*** [and more good stuff in 3:16-4:17]: Moses and God at the burning bush
8. **Exodus 12:1-14:** The first Passover
9. ***Exodus 20:1-20:*** The Ten Commandments (see also Deuteronomy 5:1-21)
10. **Numbers 11:4-30:** Grumbling in the wilderness and God providing (this is hilarious) (see also Numbers 22-24: Balaam refuses to curse Israel; Balaam's donkey)
11. ***Deuteronomy 6:1-9:*** The Great Commandment (the "Shema," Israel's basic creed)
12. **Deuteronomy 30:11-20:** "See, I have set before you life and death…choose life"

History of Israel

13. **Joshua 24:14-24:** Israel renews the covenant
    ("as for me and my house, we will serve the Lord")
14. **Judges 4:** A sample of a hero story from Judges: Deborah
15. **Ruth 1:5-18:** Ruth and Naomi (more Wisdom literature)
16. ***1 Samuel 3:*** The call of Samuel
17. **1 Samuel 16:1-13:** Samuel anoints David
18. **1 Samuel 17:** David and Goliath
19. ***2 Samuel 11- 12:23:*** David and Bathsheba
20. ***2 Samuel [18:4-15], 18:24-33:*** David mourns for his rebel son Absalom.
21. ***1 Kings 19:[1-8], 9-15:*** Elijah meets God, not in earthquake, wind or fire.
22. **2 Kings 5:1-16:** Elisha and the healing of Naaman (a foreigner)

Major Prophets:

23. ***Isaiah 6:1-8:*** Isaiah's stirring vision of the throne room of God.
24. **Isaiah 7:10-15:** The prophecy of Immanuel: God with us
25. **Isaiah 9:1-7:** "For unto us a child is born…wonderful, counselor, mighty God…"
26. **Isaiah 11:1-9:** The branch of Jesse; the peaceable kingdom
27. **Isaiah 40:1-11:** "Comfort ye my people…"
28. **Isaiah 53:** The suffering servant
29. ***Isaiah 55:*** Come, all you who are thirsty; my word will not go forth from me empty…
30. **Jeremiah 1:4-10:** The call of Jeremiah ("but I am only a child…")
31. **Jeremiah 38:** Jeremiah is thrown into a cistern, then brought out to warn the king
32. **Jeremiah 39:1-10:** Jerusalem destroyed and exiled

33. **Ezekiel 1:** The vision of the Glory of the Lord (Ezekiel saw the wheel…)
34. **Ezekiel 2 [and 3]:** The call of the prophet to speak to the exiles.
35. *****Ezekiel 37:1-14:** The vision of the valley of dry bones returned to life.
36. **Daniel 3:** Faithful men delivered from the fiery furnace.
37. **Daniel 5:** Daniel interprets the writing on the wall.
38. **Daniel 6:** faithful Daniel delivered in the lion's den.

The Minor Prophets (smaller books than the majors)

39. **Hosea 1:1-3, 2:11-3:1:** The unfaithful wife abandoned, then brought back.
40. **Joel 2:12-32:** Call a fast; the Lord's promise of redemption and his Spirit on all people.
41. *****Amos 5:21-24:** "Let justice roll down like water…"
42. **Amos 7:7-9, 8:1-7:** A plumb line and a basket of fruit: the people's injustice.
43. **Jonah 1:** Jonah tries to flee from God (and winds up in the belly of a fish)
44. **Jonah 4:** Jonah doesn't understand God's mercy.
45. *****Habakkuk 1:1-6; 2:1-3:** "How long, O Lord, how long?" God: "Write the vision…"

Poetry

46. **Psalm 1:** Their delight is in the law of the Lord…
47. **Psalm 22:** My God, my God, why have you forsaken me?
48. *****Psalm 23:** The Lord is my shepherd
49. **Psalm 51:** Have mercy on me, O God
50. *****Psalm 139:1-18:** Lord, you have searched me out and known me
51. **Psalm 150:** Praise the Lord!
52. **Song of Songs 2:** Arise, my love, my fair one

Wisdom literature

53. **Esther 4:8-16:** "Perhaps you [are here] for just such a time as this"
54. **Esther 7:2-6:** Esther finally accuses Haman
55. **Job 1 and 2:** The accuser defies God concerning Job. Job's sufferings.
56. *****Job 19:23-27:** Job's faith despite his suffering (part of Job's complaint)
57. **Job 38:1-13:** God's reply: "Where were you when I laid the foundation of the earth?"
58. **Proverbs 10:** A good sample of proverbs
59. *****Ecclesiastes 1:** "Vanity of vanities! All is vanity"
60. **Ecclesiastes 3:1-8; 12:13:** For everything there is a season; the heart of the matter

The New Testament

Parallel accounts that tell the same or similar story in other books are listed in parentheses.

Origins of Jesus:

61. *****John 1:1-18:** In the beginning was the Word…and the Word was God…
62. **Matthew 1:18-25; Luke 1:26-38:** Annunciations
63. *****Luke 2:1-21:** The birth of Jesus (wise men and infancy: Matthew 2)

Ministry:

64. **Luke 3:1-20:** John the Baptist (Mark 1:1-8, Matthew 3:1-12, John 1:6-28)
65. **Matthew 3:13-17:** Baptism of Jesus (Mark 1:9-11, Luke 3:21-22, John 1:29-34)
66. *****Luke 4:1-13:** Wilderness and Temptation (Mark 1:12-13, Matthew 4:1-11)
67. **John 2:1-11:** Wedding at Cana
68. **Matthew 4:18-22:** Call of the disciples: (Mark 1:16-20, Luke 5:1-11, John 1:35-51)

69. ***Matthew 5-7:** "Sermon on the Mount:" (Luke 5:17-6:49: "Sermon on the Plain")
70. **Matthew 13:1-53** (and in Chaps 18-25): Parables (Mark 4:1-34, 12:1-12; Luke 8:4-18, 12:13-21, and in chaps 13-18; in John, Jesus often speaks metaphorically)
71. ***Luke 15:11-32:** Parable of the Prodigal Son
72. **Luke 10:30-37:** Parable of the Good Samaritan
73. **John 11:1-44:** Raising of Lazarus
74. ***John 3:1-17:** Encounter with Nicodemus ("born again")
75. **Matthew 22:36-40:** The Summary of the Law (Mark 12:28-34, Luke10:25-28)
76. ***Mark 6:30-44:** Feeding of 5,000 (Matthew 14:13-21, Luke 9:10-17, John 6:1-15)
77. **Mark 10:46-52:** Healing of the blind (Mark 8:22-26, Matthew 20:29-34, Luke 18:35-43, John 9)
78. ***Matthew 16:13-20:** The confession of Peter (Mark 8:27-30, Luke 9:18-21)
79. **Luke 9:28-36:** The Transfiguration (Mark 9:2-8, Matthew 17:1-9)

Passion and Death:

80. **Luke 19:28-40:** Triumphal entry (Palm Sunday) (Mark 11:1-11, Matthew 21:1-11, John 12:12-19)
81. **Matthew 21:12-17:** Cleansing of the Temple (Mark 11:15-19, Luke 19:45-48, John 2:13-22)
82. **Matthew 24:29-51:** Predicting Jesus' return in glory: Mark 13:24-37, Luke 21:25-36)
83. ***Luke 22:1-38:** The Last Supper (Mark 14:12-25, Matthew 26:17-29, John 13-17)
84. **Matthew 26:30-56:** Gethsemane and arrest: (Mark 14:26-50, Luke 22:39-54, John 18:1-12)
85. **Luke 22:55-62:** Peter's denials (Mark 14:53-72, Matthew 26:57-75, John 18…)
86. ***John 18:12-19:16:** Trials (Mark 14:53-72, 15:1-15, Matthew 26:57-75, 27:1-27, Luke 22:63-71, 23:1-25)
87. ***Matthew 27:28-54:** Suffering and crucifixion (Mark 15:16-39, Luke 23:26-47, John 19:16-37)

Resurrection:

88. ***John 20:1-18:** The empty tomb (Mark 16:1-8, 9-11, Matthew 28:1-8, Luke 24:1-12)
89. **Luke 24:13-34:** The road to Emmaus (Mark 16:12 ?)
90. ***John 20:19-31:** Disciples (and Thomas) (Mark 16:12-14, Matthew 27:9-10, Luke 24:34-49)
91. ***Matthew 28:16-20:** The Great Commission (Mark 16:15, Luke 24:47, Acts 1:8, John 13:31-35)
92. **Acts 1:1-11:** Ascension (Mark 16:19)

Acts of the Apostles

93. ***Acts 2:1-18:** The coming of the Holy Spirit on Pentecost
94. **Acts 3:1-10:** Peter heals a crippled beggar
95. **Acts 8:26-40:** Philip and the Ethiopian Eunuch
96. ***Acts 9:1-18:** The Conversion of Saul (Paul)
97. **Acts 10:** Peter's vision, Cornelius and the Gentiles and their reception of the Holy Spirit
98. **Acts 15:1-21:** The Council at Jerusalem (what to do about the Gentiles)
99. **Acts 16:16-40:** Paul and Silas in Prison
100. **Acts 17:16-32:** Paul preaches to the philosophers of Athens

Letters and Revelation

101. **Romans 3:22-31:** Justification by faith rather than the law.
102. ***Romans 6:1-14:** Dead to sin and alive to Christ
103. **Romans 7:14-25:** The struggle of sin, common to all
104. **Romans 8:** Life in the Spirit; nothing can separate us from the love of God in Christ.
105. **1 Corinthians 3:** Against factions: Paul planted, Apollos watered, but God gave growth.
106. **1 Corinthians 7:1-7:** Mutuality in marriage
107. ***1 Corinthians 12:** Spiritual gifts and the unity of the Body of Christ
108. ***1 Corinthians 13:** The greatest of these is love (notice this is primarily about the church!)
109. **2 Corinthians 4:1-12; 6:3-10:** Treasures in clay jars; perseverance.
110. **Galatians 3:1-14:** You foolish Galatians! Law vs. faith.
111. **Galatians 3:26-4:7:** No divisions in Christ: Heirs of God (to whom we cry "Abba! Father!")
112. ***Galatians 5:16-26:** The fruit of sin and the fruit of the Spirit
113. ***Ephesians 4:1-16:** Many gifts to build up the body in the unity of Christ.
114. **Ephesians 5:21-6:9:** Household relationships *in Christ* (controversial, but there is more mutual submission involved than may be apparent to our 21st century ears)
115. ***Ephesians 6:10-18:** Put on the full armor of God
116. ***Philippians 2:1-11:** Make my joy complete: the humility of Christ
117. **Philippians 3:7-14; 4:4-9:** All else I count as loss; Rejoice in the Lord always!
118. **Colossians 1:15-20:** Jesus-the image of the invisible God.
119. **1 Timothy 3:1-13:** Standards for leaders in the church
120. **2 Timothy 4:1-8:** Perseverance; I've fought the good fight, run the race, kept the faith.
121. **Hebrews 11:** Those great witnesses who lived "by faith" for the promise…
122. ***Hebrews 12:1-13:** Therefore, since we are surrounded by so great a cloud of witnesses
123. ***James 1:19-27:** Be doers of the word and not merely hearers
124. **James 2:** Faith and faith in action
125. ***James 3:1-12:** Taming the tongue (or in today's world: email)
126. **1 John 1:8-2:6:** The response to sin: confession and forgiveness
127. **1 John 4:7-21:** God's love and ours
128. **Revelation 2-3:** Letters to seven churches (clean-up, persevere, be ready)
129. **Revelation 4 and 5:** The vision of the throne room of God and the lamb who was slain
130. ***Revelation 21:1-7:** The vision of the new Jerusalem

See the next page for a form that you can copy to make two double-sided bookmarks with all the above citations listed: one for the Old Testament, and one for the New Testament. Cut the paper between the two Old Testament boxes and the two and New Testament boxes. Take the pair of Old Testament lists and fold along a vertical fold between the two boxes. Tape the edges, and you will have a double-sided bookmark. Do the same for the pair of New Testament lists.

Copy this page to make two double-sided bookmarks: one for the Old Testament, and one for the New Testament.

The Bible's Greatest Hits: The Old Testament

1. *Genesis 1 & 2
2. *Genesis 3
3. Genesis 6:5-9:17
4. Genesis 12:1-7
5. Genesis 22:1-18
6. *Genesis 32:22-32
7. *Exodus 3:1-15
8. Exodus 12:1-14
9. *Exodus 20:1-20
10. Numbers 11:4-30
11. *Deuteronomy 6:1-9
12. Deuteronomy 30:11-20
13. Joshua 24:14-24
14. Judges 4
15. Ruth 1:5-18
16. *1 Samuel 3
17. 1 Samuel 16:1-13
18. 1 Samuel 17
19. *2 Samuel 11–12:23
20. *2 Samuel [18:4-15], 18-24-33
21. *1 Kings 19:[1-8], 9-15
22. 2 Kings 5:1-16
23. *Isaiah 6:1-8
24. Isaiah 7:10-15
25. Isaiah 9:1-7
26. Isaiah 11:1-9
27. Isaiah 40:1-11
28. Isaiah 53
29. *Isaiah 55
30. Jeremiah 1:4-10

The Bible's Greatest Hits: The Old Testament (continued)

31. Jeremiah 38
32. Jeremiah 39:1-10
33. Ezekiel 1
34. Ezekiel 2 [&3]
35. *Ezekiel 37:1-14
36. Daniel 3
37. Daniel 5
38. Daniel 6
39. Hosea 1:1-3, 2:11-3:1
40. Joel 2:12-32
41. *Amos 5:21-24
42. Amos 7:7-9, 8:1-7
43. Jonah 1
44. Jonah 4
45. *Habakkuk 1:1-6; 2:1-3
46. Psalm 1
47. Psalm 22
48. *Psalm 23
49. Psalm 51
50. *Psalm 139:1-18
51. Psalm 150
52. Song of Songs 2
53. Esther 4:8-16
54. Esther 7:2-6
55. Job 1 & 2
56. *Job 19:23-27
57. Job 38:1-13
58. Proverbs 10
59. *Ecclesiastes 1
60. Eccl 3:1-8; 12:13

The Bible's Greatest Hits: The New Testament

61. *John 1:1-18
62. Luke 1:26-38
63. *Luke 2:1-21
64. Luke 3:1-20
65. Matthew 3:13-17
66. Luke 4:1-13
67. John 2:1-11
68. Matthew 4:18-22
69. *Matthew 5-7
70. Matthew 13:1-53
71. *Luke 15:11-32
72. Luke 10:30-37
73. John 11:1-44
74. *John 3:1-17
75. Matthew 22:36-40
76. *Mark 6:30-44
77. Mark 10:46-52:
78. *Matthew 16:13-20
79. Luke 9:28-36
80. Luke 19:28-40
81. Matthew 21:12-17
82. Matthew 24:29-51
83. *Luke 22:1-38
84. Matthew 26:30-56
85. Luke 22:55-62
86. *John 18:12-19:16
87. *Matthew 27:28-54
88. John 20:1-18
89. Luke 24:13-34
90. *John 20:19-31
91. *Matthew 28:16-20
92. Acts 1:1-11
93. *Acts 2:1-18
94. Acts 3:1-10
95. Acts 8:26-40

The Bible's Greatest Hits: The New Testament (Continued)

96. *Acts 9:1-18
97. Acts 10
98. Acts 15:1-21
99. Acts 16:16-40
100. Acts 17:16-32
101. Romans 3:22-31
102. Romans 6:1-14
103. Romans 7:14-25
104. Romans 8
105. 1 Corinthians 3
106. 1 Corinthians 12
107. *1 Corinthians 7:1-7
108. *1 Corinthians 13
109. 2 Cor. 4:1-12; 6:3-10
110. Galatians 3:1-14
111. Galatians 3:26-4:7
112. *Galatians 5:16-26
113. *Ephesians 4:1-16
114. Ephesians 5:21-6:9
115. *Ephesians 6:10-18
116. *Philippians 2:1-11
117. Phil 3:7-14,4:4-9
118. Colossians 1:15-20
119. 1 Timothy 3:1-13
120. 2 Timothy 4:1-8
121. Hebrews 11
122. *Hebrews 12:1-13
123. *James 1:19-27
124. James 2
125. *James 3:1-12
126. 1 John 1:8-2:6
127. 1 John 4:7-21
128. Revelation 2-3
129. Revelation 4&5
130. *Revelation 21:1-7

Reading Strategies:

An introduction with five whole books of the Bible:

If you are ready to try whole books of the Bible, here is a list of five books to try in order (alternating between New Testament and Old Testament):
- Matthew: The story of Jesus
- Genesis: Creation and the ancestors of Israel
- Acts: The birth of the church
- Ruth: A short Old Testament story of fidelity
- Philippians: A New Testament letter about joy in Christ

Three two-week courses, a chapter a day:
Jesus, Paul and an intro to the Old Testament

These suggested readings come from The NRSV Student Bible, an edition with notes and resources by Philip Yancey and Tim Stafford (1996, Zondervan, pages 7-8):

Two Weeks on the Life and Teachings of Jesus

Day 1.	Luke 1: Preparing for Jesus' Arrival
Day 2.	Luke 2: the story of Jesus' birth
Day 3.	Mark 1: The beginning of Jesus' ministry
Day 4.	Mark 9: A day in the life of Jesus
Day 5.	Matthew 5: The Sermon on the Mount
Day 6.	Matthew 6: The Sermon on the Mount
Day 7.	Luke 15: Parables of Jesus
Day 8.	John 3: A conversation with Jesus
Day 9.	John 14: Jesus' final instructions
Day 10.	John 17: Jesus' final prayer for his disciples
Day 11.	Matthew 26: Betrayal and arrest
Day 12.	Matthew 27: Jesus' execution on a cross
Day 13.	John 20: Resurrection
Day 14.	Jesus' appearance after resurrection

Two Weeks on the Life and Teachings of Paul

Day 1.	Acts 9: The Conversion of Saul
Day 2.	Acts 16: Paul's Macedonian call and a jailbreak
Day 3.	Acts 17: Scenes from Paul's missionary journey
Day 4.	Acts 26: Paul tells his life story to a king
Day 5.	Acts 27: Shipwreck on the way to Rome
Day 6.	Acts 28: Paul's arrival in Rome
Day 7.	Romans 3: Paul's theology in a nutshell
Day 8.	Romans 7: Struggle with sin
Day 9.	Romans 8: Life in the Spirit
Day 10.	1 Corinthians 13: Paul's description of Love
Day 11.	1 Corinthians 15: Thoughts on the afterlife
Day 12.	Galatians 5: freedom in Christ
Day 13.	Ephesians 3: Paul's summary of his mission
Day 14.	Philippians 2: Imitating Christ

Two Weeks on the Old Testament

Day 1.	Genesis 1: The story of creation
Day 2.	Genesis 3: The origin of sin
Day 3.	Genesis 22: Abraham and Isaac
Day 4.	Exodus 3: Moses' encounter with God
Day 5.	Exodus 20: the gift of the Ten Commandments
Day 6.	1 Samuel 17: David and Goliath
Day 7.	2 Samuel 11: David and Bathsheba
Day 8.	2 Samuel 12: Nathan's rebuke of the king
Day 9.	1 Kings 18: Elijah and the prophets of Baal
Day 10.	Job 38: God's answer to Job
Day 11.	Psalm 51: A classic confession
Day 12.	Isaiah 40: words of comfort from God
Day 13.	Daniel 6: Daniel and the lions
Day 14.	Amos 4: A prophet's stern warning

Reading Strategies:

Reading Most of the Bible (Abridging the Old Testament)

If you want to read the whole Bible, but get bogged down in some of the more lengthy and hard to follow passages, here is one strategy to alleviate some of the length of the Old Testament. There are several sections that include detailed and obscure laws, genealogies, or inheritance details. Some of the tougher sections include many chapters in the prophets denouncing obscure foreign nations at great length in rambling Hebrew poetry.

In this strategy, start by reading all of the New Testament. You can read it in order, or you can start with this sequence:
- Mark
- Matthew
- John
- Luke
- Acts
- Philemon
- 1 Corinthians

Mark is the shortest Gospel account, and it is the basis for Matthew and Luke. Reading John in between Matthew and Luke will break-up the sense of repetition, and will allow Luke to flow into Acts (Acts comes from the same author as Luke). Philemon is a short letter that will get you familiar with the structure and style of Greek letters used in much of the New Testament. 1 Corinthians is a great practical letter to start with. Then turn to Romans and proceed with the rest of the New Testament in order.

The Old Testament is roughly 75% of the Bible. To relieve some of the thicker sections, **here are passages that you might omit** if the going gets slow:

- Genesis 5:1-6:8, chapter 10, 11:10-32: Genealogies
- Exodus chapters 21-31, 35-40: Legal and worship details
- Leviticus: Legal and sacrifice details
- Numbers 1-10, 26-36: Census data
- Deuteronomy 12-25: Legal details
- 1 and 2 Chronicles: A repetition of the history in 1 and 2 Kings
- Job 4-18, 20-37: Lengthy and detailed discourses on God and disaster
- Isaiah 13-33: Denouncing Gentile nations
- Jeremiah 42-51: Denouncing Gentile nations
- Ezekiel 13-23, 25-32: Denouncing Gentile nations

Once you are more familiar with the Bible, these will be worthwhile passages to read and study, (especially the ones from Job, Deuteronomy, and the prophets).

Reading Strategies:

Reading all of the Bible over one to three years:

If you are ready to tackle reading every word of the Bible, but you don't want to get bogged down in some of the thicker sections (when reading in order from Genesis to Revelation), there are several alternatives for you. You could start with the strategy above, starting with the New Testament in unique order, then reading through the Old Testament. Or you could find one of various internet tools for daily Bible reading. Or you could use one of the following tools:

"The One Year Bible" (Tyndale House, 2004):
This is a book that looks like a Bible, and contains every word of the Bible (in the NIV translation), but the material is laid out in 365 sections each to be read each day. Each day's reading includes an Old Testament reading, a New Testament reading, a Psalm and a Proverb. Sticking with this program, you will read the whole Bible in one year. Or spread the readings out into two years: Old Testament one year, and New Testament the next year. Most of the readings follow a sequence, so there is no jumping around.

Lectionaries:

Various churches and church groups have calendars of readings appointed for each week or each day. These calendars of readings are called "lectionaries." One important note is that **rarely do these lectionaries read the entire Bible**. Some are more comprehensive than others, but most of them leave out large sections. The strategy above called "Abridging the Old Testament" should provide a similar or sometimes more comprehensive approach.

Weekly Eucharistic Lectionaries:
Many churches use a weekly lectionary, based on the work of Vatican II in the 1960s. These selections follow the church year: readings about Jesus' birth at Christmas and his resurrection at Easter, for instance. These lectionaries provide readings over a three year period: Old Testament, Psalm, New Testament Epistle, and New Testament Gospel for each week. The Gospels and Epistles get fairly good coverage. The Old Testament readings tend to jump around because they are chosen to relate to the Gospel reading. The Roman Catholic Lectionary can be found at this website: http://catholic-resources.org/Lectionary/.

In recent decades, American Protestants developed a common lectionary based on the Catholic one. This is the Revised Common Lectionary (or "RCL"), which can be found on this website from Vanderbilt University: http://lectionary.library.vanderbilt.edu/

An easy to use calendar of readings from the RCL lectionary adapted for the Episcopal Church can be found on this website: http://www.lectionarypage.net/. Note that this calendar also includes readings to use when commemorating saints on particular days.

Daily Office Lectionaries:
This same tradition also provides daily readings for the cycle of prayers known as the "Daily Office" in liturgical churches (e.g. Roman Catholic, Episcopal). These are usually two-year calendars that provide for reading far more of the Bible than the Eucharistic Lectionaries. They also follow the church year, but the readings tend to stay with the same book of the Bible and read in sequence. Searching the internet based on "Daily Office lectionary" will yield a myriad of websites and web tools for daily Bible reading. See more in the Bibliography on page 75.

Bibliography

Bibles:

The NIV Study Bible, Kenneth Barker, ed., Grand Rapids: Zondervan, 1995.
See also the 2011 edition. Includes introductions, indexes, maps, timelines, and explanatory footnotes. The NIV does NOT include the Apocrypha.

The Quest Study Bible (NIV), Marshall Shelly, ed., Grand Rapids: Zondervan, 1994.
There are newer editions. Includes introductions, indexes, maps, timelines, and explanatory margin notes. More extensive notes and more question-oriented than the NIV Study Bible. The NIV does NOT include the Apocrypha.

The One Year Bible (NIV), Carol Stream, IL: Tyndale House Publishers, Inc., 2004.
Assigns readings from the Bible to each day of the year so that you finish the whole Bible in one year. Uses the NIV translation.

The NRSV Student Bible, Phillip Yancey and Tim Stafford, eds, Grand Rapids: Zondervan, 1996.
Notes in this edition are designed more for devotion and elaboration than for technical detail. Lots of introductory material. This edition does NOT include the Apocrypha.

The New Oxford Annotated Bible (NRSV), Bruce Metzger and Roland Murphy, ed., New York: Oxford University Press, third edition, 2001.
More scholarly and dry in its notes. Includes the Apocrypha.

The Holy Bible, English Standard Version (ESV), Wheaton, IL: Crossway, 2001.

For the translation of the Psalms used in this book, see:
The Book of Common Prayer, New York: Church Publishing, 1979.

Other helpful texts:

Brown, Raymond E. *Introduction to the New Testament*. New York: Doubleday, 1997.
A well-organized scholarly introduction. Includes discussions of special topics, and summaries, outlines and introductions to each book. Written at a college-level.

Longman, Tremper III, and Raymond B. Dillard. *Introduction to the Old Testament.* Grand Rapids: Zondervan, 2006.

Goldingay, John. *Old Testament for Everyone (Series)*. Louisville, KY: Westminster John Knox Press, 2010.
A companion to Wright's New Testament for Everyone series.

Wright, N.T. *New Testament for Everyone (Series)*. Louisville, KY: Westminster John Knox Press, 2011.
This series of commentaries is written by a leading New Testament scholar. These books are rich in content, but delivered in a style and manner that is easily accessible to the Biblical novice. I highly recommend this series and this author.

Websites for Bible Studies and Lectionaries:

Bible Gateway: www.biblegateway.com
A simple, free online search engine for the Bible.

Bible Resources.org: http://bibleresources.org/
An evangelical resource page.

Revised Common Lectionary: http://lectionary.library.vanderbilt.edu/
A Protestant calendar of scripture readings for Sundays, used in many churches. See also www.lectionarypage.net for the weekly calendar of readings for the Episcopal Church, based on the Revised Common Lectionary.

Roman Catholic Lectionary: http://catholic-resources.org/Lectionary/
A Roman Catholic calendar of scripture readings for Sundays.

The Daily Office lectionary in blog style, using the ESV: http://feeds.feedburner.com/ESV-bcp
Uses the daily lectionary from the Episcopal Church's Book of Common Prayer.

Daily and Weekly Lectionaries
www.presbyterianmission.org/ministries/devotions/month-month-lectionary-reading-list/
From the Presbyterians (based on the Revised Common Lectionary for weekly and the Book of Common Prayer for daily readings).

Roman Catholic daily readings: www.usccb.org/bible/readings

Online Book of Common Prayer (Episcopal Church): www.bcponline.org
For prayers and psalms.

Blue Kayak Publishing: www.bluekayakpublishing.com
Publishers of "A Tour of the Bible" and other resources for the church, including free online resources.

Software for word and language study:

Bible Works: www.bibleworks.com

Logos: www.logos.com

Accordance: www.accordancebible.com

Glossary

Agape: One of the Greek words for love, meaning self-giving love. Pronounced "a-GAH-pay."

Anoint: To pour oil on; Kings in ancient Israel were not crowned, they were anointed with oil. The *Messiah* means the anointed one--God's chosen king.

Apocalyptic: A kind of literature characterized by wild symbolic visions of the battle of the forces of evil and the victorious forces of God. See Daniel, Zechariah and Revelation.

Apocrypha: Name given by Protestants to Jewish literature that some Christians consider part of the Bible, but Protestants do not. See pages 38-39, and 61. Also called "Deutero-canonical books."

Apostles: From the word meaning "one who is commissioned," The Apostles were twelve of Jesus' disciples who formed an inner circle of leaders around Jesus.

Aramaic: Language similar to Hebrew spoken by many Jews in the Middle East at the time of Jesus (Hebrew was seldom spoken by that time).

Ascension: After Jesus rose from the dead and spoke with his disciples, he departed from them (but did not die). They saw him rise into the sky, and called this his "ascension into heaven." This is not space travel, but rather Jesus left to the presence of God the Father.

Assyria: An ancient empire to the north of Israel, with its capital city of Nineveh (see page 19). Assyria destroyed the northern Kingdom of Israel and scattered its people in 721 BC.

Baal: A fertility god worshiped by various peoples around Israel. Prophets spoke out against the Israelites (or their kings) for worshipping or allowing the worship of Baal. Usually pronounced in English like the word "bail."

Babylon: An ancient Empire to the northeast of Israel, in present day Iraq. (see page 19). Bablylon (under King Nebuchadnezzar) destroyed Judah, including Jerusalem and its Temple in 587 BC.

Blasphemy: Speech that insults or dishonors God. Jesus was tried for blasphemy since he called himself God.

Born again: A translation of a phrase in Greek in John 3:1-21. The phrase has a double meaning: "born again" or "born from above." Jesus uses this double meaning to teach about having a new life through faith in him.

Canaan: The land that is now generally described as Israel and Palestine. This name was used prior to the Israelites settling in the land after the exodus from Egypt.

Canon: Means the authoritative text. The "canon of scripture" is the particular selection of texts that are considered authoritative to a religion—the writings that are considered the official Bible.

Catholic: "Of the whole;" originally used to describe the beliefs held in common by all Christians, now it commonly applies to the Roman Catholic Church. Other churches may describe themselves as catholic in their beliefs.

Charity: Used in the King James Version of the Bible to translate one of the Greek words for love (*agape*--see above). This originally described self-giving love.

Chesed: See "Loving-kindness" and "Steadfast-Love" on page 13.

Church: In the New Testament, this word translates a Greek word meaning "assembly." The church is the Christian community more so than a building.

Covenant: A contract or agreement or promise, but usually with wider and more permanent implications. See page 13.

Crucifixion: Execution by hanging on a large cross. Death comes by losing breath due to the position of the body and prolonged weakness.

Deutero-cannonical books: See Apocrypha above.

Devil: An evil spiritual creature opposed to God. The title of a particular evil spirit, also called Satan (see below).

Diaspora: Scattering or dispersion, usually of a people or ethnic group. The most commonly discussed diaspora is when Rome destroyed Jerusalem in 70AD, dispersing Jews throughout the empire. Also applies to Jews/Israelis living outside Judah/Israel after being conquered by Babylon or Assyria.

Disciple: a student/follower of a teacher/leader (and who then teach/lead other disciples). Jesus had many disciples; the twelve leaders among them were called "Apostles."

Doctrine: A religious belief, usually an official explanation of a religious claim.

Editions of the Bible: Translations of the Bible can be packaged into various editions that add footnotes, maps, and commentary, usually tailored for a particular audience. The additions are not part of the Bible. One translation of the Bible can be published in various editions. See p. 58-59.

Epistle: A fancy word for "letter," now usually only referring to letters written by Apostles to churches or people, later included in the New Testament.

Evangelist: Someone who preaches the "Gospel" or "Good News," the story and message of Jesus. In Biblical studies, the title "Evangelist" is particularly used to refer to the authors of the four accounts of the Gospel: Matthew, Mark, Luke and John.

Exile: Being taken away from one's home country. In the Bible, the chief exile is when Babylon destroyed Jerusalem and took most of the people back to Babylon to live.

Exodus: The departure of the Hebrews from slavery in Egypt. Also the title of the Biblical book that tells the story.

Faith: In the Bible, faith is usually a combination of trust in God, belief in God and loyalty to God, rooted in relationship with God.

Former Prophets: Usually describes the books of the Bible of Judges, Samuel and Kings. Also describes significant prophets from these books: Samuel, Nathan, Elijah, and Elisha. Distinguished from "Latter Prophets" (see below).

Genres: Styles or types of literature (poetry, story, law, history, parable, etc). See "Form Criticism," page 62, and a sampling of Biblical genres on page 11.

Gentile: Non-Jews or the nations around Israel—those who worshipped other gods. The same Hebrew word can be translated "Gentiles" or "nations."

Glory of the Lord: A phrase that describes the presence of God, often in a burning radiance shrouded by smoke or cloud. Used especially in Exodus, Numbers, Ezekiel, Psalms and Isaiah.

Gnosticism: A secretive religion that developed ~150-250 AD, based on "secret knowledge" (*gnosis* is the Greek word for "knowledge"). It used some Christian ideas, but with very different meanings. See page 61.

Gospel: The "Good News" of the story and message of Jesus (forgiveness of sins, promise of new and eternal life in him, promise of the resurrection from the dead). Also describes the books of the Bible that tell the basic story of Jesus (Matthew, Mark, Luke and John).

Grace: A gift freely given (not deserved). God's grace is his favor to us, undeserved and unearned.

Greatest Hits: A name that *A Tour of the Bible* gives to particularly well-known, influential, memorable or representative passages of the Bible. They were selected by the author with this general criteria, without a specific science involved…

Hell: Eternal separation from God, seen as eternal torment. Jesus saves us from this hell. See Luke 12:5, Matthew 25:31-46.

Hermeneutic: An approach to understanding the meaning of scripture, based on factors such as culture or philosophical approach. For instance, Christians and Jews may interpret the Old Testament differently—they use different hermeneutics. See page 62.

Holiness/Holy: A quality related to God: sacred, set apart for God, set apart by God, a proper approach to God in worship (see "holiness codes" in Leviticus).

Holy Spirit: The power and presence of God in the world. The doctrine of the Trinity describes God the Holy Spirit as one with God the Father and God the Son (Jesus).

Household codes: Descriptions of how a household should be structured rightly (relationships between parents and children, husbands and wives, masters and servants or slaves). See Ephesians on p. 52.

Imprecatory psalms: Psalms that ask for God's aid against enemies. See pages 21 and 22.

Israel: The name God gave Jacob (Abraham's grandson), meaning "one who wrestles with God." The people descended from Jacob (in twelve tribes). The nation that united the twelve tribes, or later in its history, the northern kingdom of ten of the tribes (separated from the Kingdom of Judah in the south). The capital of the northern kingdom was Samaria.

Jehovah: A rendering of the name of God from the Old Testament. Its spelling is based on a mistake in translation from the Hebrew. See "The LORD," page 12.

Judges: A book in the Bible that describes a time when the tribes of Israel lived in a loose confederation—before there were kings. Periodically, the tribes were united by heroes of the people. These heroes are called judges in the Bible, though only one (Deborah) is described as deciding disputes. See page 20.

King James Version: Also called the "Authorized Version," this is an early and highly influential English translation of the Bible commissioned by King James I in England in 1611. Known for using older pronouns such as "thee" and "thou." See page 58. Sometimes abbreviated as "KJV."

Kingdom of God: Jesus preached about the Kingdom of God to describe what it is like to live under God's reign, now influencing the world, and coming in its fullness when Jesus returns.

Kingdom of Heaven: See "Kingdom of God;" the phrase used in Matthew instead of Kingdom of God.

Lamentations: A kind of literature expressing intense sadness and loss (and a book of the Bible by the same name, lamenting the destruction of Jerusalem by Babylon).

Latter Prophets: Prophetic books of Isaiah, Jeremiah, Ezekiel, Daniel and the 12 "Minor Prophets." These are distinguished from the "Former Prophets" (see above), as these prophets have books named for them and are primarily about their ministry.

Lectionary: A calendar of readings of scripture assigned to each week or each day. See page 73.

Licentious: An attitude that behavior is not limited by rules or a moral code; free to sin.

Logos: One of the Greek words for "word," usually implying a word with power. Used in Plato's philosophy to describe the word of the eternal god who created the world through his Logos (his "word"). John and later Christianity used this philosophy to describe Jesus as the eternal Logos of God (the Word of God in a human person). See John chapter 1.

LORD: A rendering of the name of God from the Old Testament. See "The LORD," page 12.

Maccabees: The family of those who led a Jewish rebellion against Greek rulers in 167 BC. They established Jewish independence for a century, often called the Hasmonean period. See page 10, 39. The title of a book of the Apocrypha describing this period.

Major Prophets: The prophetic books of the Old Testament that are large in size (Isaiah, Jeremiah, Ezekiel, Daniel). In contrast to the smaller "Minor Prophets" (see below). See pages 32-33.

Manna: Special food from heaven ("bread from heaven") given by God to the people of Israel as they journeyed in the wilderness in between leaving Egypt and settling in the Promised Land (Canaan). They found manna on the ground in the mornings.
Mesopotamia: The land of the Tigris and Euphrates river valleys, in present day Iraq. The cradle of ancient civilization and the home of Babylon.
Messiah: God's "anointed" (kings in Israel were anointed with oil, not crowned). The prophets foretold that God's Messiah would come to renew Israel. A title of Jesus (though most Jews today don't agree that he is the Messiah).
Minor Prophets: The last twelve books of the Old Testament in most Bibles, these are prophetic books much smaller in size than the "Major Prophets" (see above). See pages 32-33.
Moab: A neighboring nation to Israel, who worshipped the god Molech.
Modernism: A world view that finds truth in what is scientifically verifiable and repeatable. This view tends to discount or disbelieve in anything supernatural or miraculous.
See page 64.
Nations: In the Old Testament, the Hebrew word for "nations" is the same word translated "Gentiles."
New Testament: The newer, second section of the Bible with the story of Jesus and his disciples. ~25% of the volume of the Bible. See pages 8 and 9.
Old Testament: The older, first section of the Bible with the story of God's relationship with the descendants of Abraham (the people of Israel). ~75% of the volume of the Bible.
See pages 8 and 9.
Orthodox: Meaning "right worship" or "right belief." This word became associated with the church in eastern Europe, Asia and certain places in North Africa ("Eastern Orthodox" churches).
Parable: A story with a deeper meaning. Jesus taught with parables, using them especially to describe the Kingdom of God, God's character, or our relationship with God.
See page 42.
Paraphrase: Rephrasing a statement without using the same words. Some translations of the Bible are paraphrases, meaning that the translators are seeking to translate more loosely their understanding of the meaning of the passage, rather than holding tightly to a more word-for-word translation approach.
Passover: The Jewish holiday commemorating God's deliverance of the Israelites from slavery in Egypt. The final plague sent by God on the Egyptians was death, but the angel of death passed over the homes of the Hebrews (their homes were marked with blood from a lamb slaughtered for that night's meal). Christians describe Jesus' death as a Passover lamb's death that saves us from death. See Exodus 12:1-14.
Patriarch: A chief father of a family. Used to describe the first ancestors of the Israelites: Abraham, Isaac and Jacob.
Pentecost: A Jewish holiday celebrating God giving the law to Moses. Also a Christian holiday celebrating God giving the Holy Spirit to the disciples after Jesus' death, resurrection and ascension (this gift of the Holy Spirit happened on the feast of Pentecost).
Persecution: Undeserved mistreatment, sometimes violent. The Jews were persecuted, and the Christians were persecuted as well.
Pharisees: One of several groups of Jewish religious leaders in the days of Jesus. The Pharisees were teachers of the Torah, and after Rome destroyed the Temple, they sustained Judaism in the Empire through the Synagogue system (Jewish communities outside Jerusalem). The Pharisees were opposed to Jesus, and Jesus often criticized they way they applied the law (especially in cases of hypocrisy).

Pharaoh: The title of the king of Egypt.
Philistines: A people living on the Mediterranean coast adjacent to Judah; they were frequent enemies of the people of Israel in Old Testament times.
Poetry: See pages 24-27 on Hebrew Poetry.
Pontius Pilate: Roman governor of the region around Jerusalem at the time of Jesus. He ordered Jesus' crucifixion.
Post-Modern: A world-view in contrast to Modernism (see above), arising in the 20th century. Where Modernism sought only solid certainty in facts, Post-modernism is more comfortable with mystery, and recognizes the influence of bias and perception on all philosophical truth claims. In extremes, Post-modernism claims multiple "truths." See page 64.
Prophet: Primarily, a prophet is one who speaks a message from God ("thus says the Lord:…"). Also the title of Biblical books by or about certain prophets. See page 35.
Protestant: Christian churches that developed from churches that broke with the Roman Catholic Church in Europe in the 1500s.
Proverbs: Short statements of wisdom, written in Hebrew poetry; The Old Testament book of Proverbs.
Psalms: The Old Testament book where each chapter is an individual psalm. Psalms are Hebrew poetry. See pages 24-29.
Purim: Jewish holiday celebrating Esther's actions to save Jews in Persia. See page 22.
Resurrection: Rising from the dead; Jesus' resurrection, or the resurrection of the dead at Jesus' second coming
Sacrifice: Worship of a god by giving up something, usually burning an animal, often as a price paid for a sin or offense, or an offering to gain a god's favor.
Samaritans: Descendants of the northern kingdom of Israel (which was destroyed by Assyria). Jews of Jesus' day often criticized the Samaritans for a reputation of inter-marrying with pagans.
Satan: "the accuser" in Hebrew. Appears in Job to accuse Job before God. Identified with the Devil, the one who tempts Jesus in the wilderness to turn away from God.
Second Coming: When Jesus will return to earth, raise the dead, judge the world, conquer evil and establish his kingdom in its fullness. See Revelation, 1 Thessalonians, and Jesus' predictions (under "suffering and death" on page 41).
Septuagint: A translation of Jewish scriptures into Greek made before the time of Christ. This was the most common "Bible" for Jews of that day and the basis of the Old Testament for Christians. See page 60.
Shema: Deuteronomy 6:4-5. The Hebrew word that begins this passage is *shema*, which means hear or listen. This is Israel's basic creed. See page 16.
Son of God: One of the titles of Jesus, indicating that he came from God and is one with God the Father.
Son of Man: One of the titles of Jesus, referring to passages in Daniel about the Messiah—the one who would come from God to set things right.
Sovereignty: Authority over; God's sovereignty is his authority over all things.
Speaking in tongues: The gift of the Holy Spirit to speak in other languages (otherwise unknown to the person). See Acts 2, and 1 Corinthians 12. Often experienced as a gift of prayer.
Steadfast love: Also Covenant-love-and-faithfulness or loving-kindness. A way of translating the Hebrew word *chesed*. See page 13.

Synagogue: A gathering of Jews outside of Jerusalem—gathering to pray, read scriptures and teach and learn.

Synoptic: The title given to the New Testament books of Matthew, Mark and Luke. They are very similar and use a similar chronology (whereas John tells the story a little differently). Synoptic means "from the same eyes." See page 43.

Temple (in Jerusalem): The central place where God was to be worshipped by the people of Israel. Built by Solomon, it signified the place of God's presence. Its destruction by Babylon was devastating. Jews rebuilt the temple years later, and it was enlarged by King Herod in Roman times. Rome destroyed this new temple in 70 AD.

Torah: Meaning "law" or "instruction," this is the section of the Bible with the first five books: Genesis, Exodus, Leviticus, Numbers, and Deuteronomy. See pages 14-17.

Translations of the Bible: The Bible books were originally written in Hebrew (Old Testament) and Greek (New Testament). There are multiple ways to translate these texts into English, so there are several different English translations of the Bible. See pages 58-59.

Trinity: The Christian Doctrine that God is one God, but "in three persons:" God the Father, God the Son (Jesus) and God the Holy Spirit. Each is God, but there is only one God, not three. Often described by Christians as a mystery. See page 47.

Twelve Tribes of Israel: Tribes each descended from one of Jacob's twelve sons. See page 17.

Womanist: An approach to interpreting scripture (or history or other texts) based on the point of view of third world women. Womanist perspectives developed as a reaction by some who claimed that Feminism represents a view of white women from the developed world.

Word (*logos*): See "*Logos*" above.

Word of God: Jesus is called the "Word of God" (see "*Logos*" above). The Bible is called the Word of God because its writers were uniquely inspired by the Holy Spirit. See page 5.

Writings: Books in the Old Testament not part of the Torah or the Prophets. Writings contain history, poetry and wisdom literature. See page 8.

Yahweh: A rendering of the name of God from the Old Testament. See "The Lord," page 12.

Index

(page numbers in bold indicate pages where this item is a principal subject)

Abel: 15
Abraham: 8, 10, 12-15, 17, 48, 65, 66, 71.
Abram : (see Abraham)
Absalom: 18, 21, 66.
Acts of the Apostles: 2, 3, 7, 9, 41, 44, 45, **46, 47,** 50, 65, 68, 70-72.
Adam: 14, 15.
Ahab: 18, 22, 23, 33.
Amnon: 21
Amos: 2, 23, 26, **33, 34, 37,** 65, 67, 70, 71.
Apocalyptic: 9, 11, 32, 33, 35-37, 39, 56, 76.
Apocrypha: 2, 3, 9, 30, 31, **38, 39,** 60, **61,** 76.
Apostle: 8, 9, 33, 37, 42, 45, **46-47,** 56, 76.
Assyria: 8, 10, 19, 22, 23, 32, 33, 35, 37, 38, 76.
Babylon: 8, 10, 19, 22, 23, 32, 35-37, 56, 76.
Balaam: 14, 66.
Baruch: 2, **38, 39.**
Bathsheba: 18, 21, 33, 66.
Bel and the Dragon: 2, **39.**
Cain: 15
Canon: 2, 5, 9, 31, 38, 39, **60-61,** 62, 63, 76.
Catholic (Roman): 9, 38, 39, 59, 61, 73, 76.
Chesed: **13,** 33, 76.
Chronicles: 2, 3, 8, **18-19, 22,** 39.
Colossians: 2, **48, 49, 52,** 69, 70.
Corinthians: 2, 3, 13, **48-51,** 65, 69-72.
Covenant: 8, **13,** 14-16, 18, 19, 22, 36, 37, 66, 76.
Creation: 6, 7, 10, 11, 13, 14, 15, 50, 64, 65, 66, 70, 71.
Daniel: 2, 3, 8, 23, 25, 31, **32, 34,** 35, **36,** 38, 39, 56, 67, 70, 71.
David: 8, 10, **18-21,** 22, 23, 28, 30, 39, 42, 65, 66, 71.
Deborah: 18, **20,** 27, 66.
Deutero-cannonical books: See Apocrypha
Deuteronomy: 2, 3, 8, **14-16,** 66, 70, 72.
Disciple: 8, 38, 41, 42, 45, 46, 50, 53, 61, 67, 68, 71, 77.
Ecclesiastes: 2, 3, 8, 11, 25, 27, **30, 31,** 67, 70.
Ecclesiasticus: 2, 30, 31, **39.**
Elijah: 17-19, 22, 33, 66, 71.

Elisha: 17-19, 22, 33, 66.
Ephesians: 2, **48-50, 52,** 69-71.
Epistle: (see also Letter) 9, 50, 53, 55, 73.
Esau: 15, 17.
Esdras: 2, **39.**
Esther: 2, 3, 8, **18-22, 30, 31,** 38, 67, 70.
Eve: 14, 15.
Exodus: 2, 3, 8, 10, 13, **14-16,** 24, 27, 30, 65, 66, 70-72, 77.
Ezekiel: 2, 3, 8, 13, 23, 25, **32,** 34, 35, **36,** 65, 66, 67, 70, 72.
Ezra: 2, 3, 8, 10, **18-19, 22,** 23, 39.
Galatians: 2, **48-51,** 65, 69-71.
Genesis: 2, 3, 4, 6-8, 11, 13, **14-16,** 62, 64-66, 70-73.
Genres of Biblical literature: 3, 11, 22, 25, 30, **62,** 77.
Gentile: 12, 32, 33, 36-38, 43, 45-47, 50-52, 68, 72, 77.
Gideon: 18, **20.**
Gnosticism: 55, 61, 77.
Gospel: 2, 3, 9, 10, 12, 13, **40-46,** 50, 55, 56, 60, 64, 72, 73, 77.
Habakkuk: 2, 23, **33, 34, 37,** 67, 70.
Hagar: 15, 17.
Haggai: 2, 23, **33, 34, 37.**
Haman: 18, 22, 30, 38, 67.
Hebrews (book): 2, 3, **54, 59,** 69, 70.
Hell: 77.
Holy Spirit: 4, 5, 9, 33, 37, 42, 43, 45, **46-47,** 51, 63, 68, 78, 79, 80, 81.
Hosea: 2, 23, **33, 34, 36,** 37, 67, 70.
"I am": **12**
Isaac: 8, 10, 12, 14, 15, 17, 66, 71.
Isaiah: 2, 3, 8, 23, 26, **32, 34, 35,** 37, 65, 66, 70-72.
Ishmael: 15, 17.
Israel: (see also Jacob), 3, 5, 8, 10, **12-23,** 30, 33, 35-38, 42, 43, 50, 57, 60, 66, 77, **Inner Front Cover**.
Jacob: 8, 10, 12, 14-17, 66.
James (book): 2, 3, **54, 55,** 69, 70.
Jehovah: 12, 59, 77.
Jeremiah: 2, 3, 8, 11, 23, **32, 34,** 35, **36,** 39, 65, 66, 70, 72.

Jeremiah (Letter of): 2, **39.**
Jericho: 20
Jerusalem: 10, 19, 22-24, 26, 33-37, 39, 42, 44-47, 51, 55, 56, 59, 65, 66, 68, 69.
Jesus: 5, 7-10, 12, 13, 20, 30, 35, 36, 38, 39, **40-43,** 45-47, 49-52, 55, 56, 58-61, 64, 67-69, 71, 73.
Jezebel: 22, 23, 33.
Job: 2, 3, 8, 25, 27, **30, 31,** 70-72.
Joel: 2, 23, **33, 34,** 35, **37,** 67, 70.
John: 2, 3, 6, 9, 10, 12, 13, **40, 41,** 43, **45,** 56, 60, 65, 67, 68, 70-72.
John (Letters 1, 2, and 3): 2, 3, **54, 55,** 56, 70.
John the Baptist: 40-42, 44, 45, 67.
Jonah: 2, 25, 31, **33, 34, 37,** 67, 70.
Joseph: 14, 15, **16,** 17, 20, 66.
Joshua: 2, 3, 8, 16, **18-20,** 35, 66, 70.
Josiah: 19, 22, 23, 39.
Jude: 2, 3, **54, 55.**
Judges: 2, 3, 8, 10, **18-20,** 25, 30, 66, 70, 78.
Judith: 2, **38.**
King James Version: 6, 13, 38, **58,** 59, 78.
Kingdom of God: 42-44, 64, 78.
Kingdom of Heaven: 44, 78.
Kings: 2, 3, 8, 10, 11, **18-21,** 22, **23,** 31, 32, 35, 36, 42, 66, 70, 71, 72.
Lamentations: 2, 3, 8, **24,** 25, 78.
Leah: 15, 17.
Lectionary: 73, 78.
Letter: (see also Epistle) 2, 3, 7, 9-12, 39, 45, 47, **48-55,** 56, 60, 61, 69, 71, 72.
Leviticus: 2, 3, 8, 11, **14-16,** 72.
The Lord: 11, **12,** 13, 15, 16, 18-20, 22, 24-31, 33-37, 43, 49, 52, 55, 59, 60, 66, 67.
Love: **13,** 16, 24, 25, 27, 33, 34, 37, 45, 48-52, 54, 55, 58, 67, 69, 71.
Luke: 2, 3, 9, **40, 41,** 43, 44, **45,** 46, 60, 65, 67, 70-72.
Maccabees: 2, 23, **38, 39,** 78.
Malachi: 2, 23, **33, 34, 37.**
Manasseh: 2, **39.**
Mark: 2, 3, 6, 7, 9, 11, **40, 41,** 43, **44,** 45, 60, 66-72.
Matthew: 2, 3, 7, 9, 11, **40, 41,** 43, **44,** 45, 60, 65, 67, 68, 70-72.
Messiah: **13,** 26, 35, 37, 40, 42-45, 79.
Micah: 2, 23, **33, 34, 37.**

Moab: 18, 20, 30, Inner Front Cover, 79.
Modernism: 62, **64,** 79.
Moses: 8, 12, **14-16,** 22, 24, 27, 43, 44, 65, 66, 71.
Nahum: 2, 23, **33, 34, 37.**
Naomi: 18, 20, 30, 66.
Nathan: 21, 23, 33, 71.
Nations: **12,** 25, 32, 33, 35-38, 72, 79.
Nehemiah: 2, 3, 8, 10, **18-19, 22,** 23, 39.
Noah: 13, 14, **15,** 66.
Numbers: 2, 3, 8, **14-16,** 66, 70, 72.
Obadiah: 2, 23, **33, 37.**
Orthodox: 2, 9, 38, 39, 61, 79.
Patriarch: 8, 10, 14, 15, 79.
Paul: (see also Saul(Paul)), 2, 3, 7, 9, 13, **45-53,** 55, 60, 65, 68-71.
Persia: 10, 19, 22, 23, 30, 36.
Peter (books): 2, 3, **54, 55.**
Pharaoh: 16, 79.
Philemon: 2, 3, 11, **49, 50,** 52, **53.**
Philippians: 2, 7, **48, 49, 52,** 69-71.
Philistines: 20, 79, Inner Front Cover.
Poetry: 2, 3, 6, 8, **24-27,** 31, 35, 38, 39, 62, 67, 72, 80.
Post-Modern: 64, 80.
Prophet (books): 2, 3, 6, 8, 22-26, 31, 32-37, 60, 66, 67, 72.
Prophet (people): 3, 8, 10, 13, 19-23, 31, 32-**37,** 39, 42, 65-67, 71, 72, 80.
Protestant: 9, 38, 39, 59, 61, 73, 80.
Proverbs: 2, 3, 8, 11, 25, 27, **30, 31,** 38, 39, 67, 70, 80.
Psalms: 2, 3, 8, **24,** 25, **28-29,** 31, 39, 67, 70, 71, 80.
Rachel: 15, 17.
Reading Strategies: 3, 4, 6, 7, 42, 57, **65-73.**
Rebekah: 17
Resurrection: 5, 9, 10, 36, 40-45, 49-52, 65, 68, 71, 73, 80.
Revelation: 2, 3, 9, 10, 11, 37, **56,** 60, 65, 69, 70, 73.
Romans: 2, 3, 11, 43, **48-50,** 51, 69-72
Ruth: 2, 3, 7, 8, **18-20,** 22, 30, 31, 66, 70, 71.
Samson: 18, 20.
Samuel: 2, 3, 8, **18-21,** 22, 23, 27, 65, 66, 70, 71.

Sarah: 14, 15, 17, 38.
Sarai: (see Sarah)
Saul (King): 10, 19, **20,** 23, 27, 33.
Saul (Paul): 46, 47, 68, 71
Second Coming: 40, 42, 49, 52, 54.
Sexual morality: 48, 49.
Sirach: see Ecclesiasticus
Slave/slavery: 8, 10, **13,** 15, 16, 48, 49, 51, 53, 59, 62.
Solomon: 8, 10, 18, 19, 22-24, 31, 38,
Son of God: 42, 43, 45, 80.
Son of Man: 36, 42, 80.
Song of Solomon: see Song of Songs
Song of Songs: 2, 3, 8, **24,** 25, 67, 70.
Song of the Three Jews: 2, **39.**
Susanna: 2, **39.**
Synoptic: 43-45, 81.

Tamar: 21
Thessalonians: 2, **49, 52.**
Timothy: 2, **49, 50, 53,** 69, 70.
Titus: 2, **49, 50, 53.**
Tobit: 2, 31, **38.**
Torah: 2, 3, 8, **14-16,** 19, 31, 44, 51, 60, 66.
Translations of the Bible: 3-6, 12, 38, 57, **58-59,** 60, 61, 81.
Trinity: 5, 47, 81.
Twelve Tribes of Israel: 12, **16, 17,** 18-20, 81.
Uriah: 21
Wisdom: 2, 30, 31, **38, 39.**
Word *(logos)*: 12, **13,** 41, 45, 81.
Word of God: 5, 9, 13, 38, 60, 61, 81.
Zechariah: 2, 23, **33, 34, 37.**
Zephaniah: 2, 23, **33, 34, 37.**

www.ingramcontent.com/pod-product-compliance
Lightning Source LLC
Chambersburg PA
CBHW061818290426
44110CB00026B/2913